eat greens

Seasonal Recipes to Enjoy in Abundance

by Barbara Scott-Goodman & Liz Trovato

RUNNING PRESS
PHILADELPHIA • LONDON

9 8 7 6 5 4 3 2 1

Digit on the right indicates the number of this printing

Library of Congress Control Number: 2010932340

ISBN 978-0-7624-3907-2

Food Photography: Colin Cooke
Garden Photography: Charles Clough
Food Stylist: Ulf Aggers
Cover design: Barbara Scott-Goodman
Interior Design: Barbara Scott-Goodman and Liz Trovato
Typography: MetaPlus

Running Press Book Publishers
2300 Chestnut Street
Philadelphia, PA 19103-4371
Visit us on the web!
www.runningpresscooks.com

To the farmers and the gardeners all over the country,
who grow the good stuff and get it to our tables.
BS-G

To the memory of my aunt, Cissy Trumbull,
who grew the best Swiss chard on earth.
LT

contents

introduction

There may be a few good reasons why you are reading this book. Perhaps you have your own garden and want to explore new ways to prepare all the wonderful, plentiful green vegetables that you grow. Or you may be a novice to greens and are curious about how to expand your cooking repertoire and prepare the lovely produce that you see when shopping at your local farmers' market. Or maybe you are someone who wants to eat healthier foods and incorporate more greens into your diet as well as your family's. These are all excellent reasons to read and enjoy this book.

We love the pure and simple pleasure of growing, cooking, and eating greens. And fortunately, greens of all varieties are increasingly available at produce stands, farmers' markets, and supermarkets all around the country. People's eyes have been opened to the greatness of greens, and they are ready and willing to try new recipes and experiment with fresh produce that they are not necessarily familiar with. The popularity of greens is part of a general rediscovery of the joys of the real, earthy flavors and visual beauty found in fresh, seasonal produce.

Our approach to cooking greens is, "Get in the garden or go to the market, then decide what to cook." We seek out the best-quality, freshest produce that we can find in the garden, at farmers' markets, and in grocery stores. When we developed the recipes for this book we didn't consider these vegetables to be merely side dishes or afterthoughts to the main event. We cooked up a range of fantastic appetizers, soups, salads, and main dishes as well. We steamed, sautéed, stir-fried, braised, roasted, and blanched all manner of greens with delicious results. Of course, we cooked them with the usual suspects—olive oil, garlic, and lemon—but we also experimented with a range of other ingredients, such as ginger, chiles, anchovies, flavored oils, nuts, and sausages, and found that they work beautifully with and enhance the flavors of greens.

Not only do greens have wonderful and intriguing flavors, they are also very good for you and should be incorporated into everyone's diet. Fresh greens contain high amounts of vitamins C and E and beta-carotene, which are antioxidants that may possibly prevent

cancer. They also have high amounts of essential minerals, particularly iron and calcium, and they improve immunity function. So it turns out that your mom was right when she said, "Eat your greens."

Another great asset of greens is that they are so versatile and flexible to cook with. Whatever greens are used in a given recipe, you should always feel free to substitute and adapt according to what is available and to your own taste. Herbed Leek and Watercress Soup is just fine with another green if there is no watercress to be found at the market or if you've just picked some fresh chard from the garden and want to add that instead. The same goes for Mixed Greens Gumbo, Kale, Sweet Potato, and Orzo Soup, or Swiss Chard Frittata. There are no hard and fast rules for cooking greens; you just need to use the freshest and best tasting ones you can find.

We hope that you use and enjoy this book and cook everything in it from artichokes to zucchini. May all of our tables be abundant with fresh, gorgeous greens!

liz's garden notes on growing greens

If you are lucky enough to have a nice sunny spot in your yard, patio, or deck, put up a raised bed and fill it with greens. I am a lazy gardener, so I prefer my beds right close to my back door so I can observe the daily changes, and so I don't have to stray too far from my kitchen. They not only provide a lovely contrast to other flowering plants with the many different shades of green, but they are surprisingly easy to grow. I lived in New York City for forty years, and I killed many a houseplant there. People who know me can't believe that I can get anything to stay alive, much less grow. If I can do it, you can do it. I kid you not.

Arugula flourishes in planters, as does basil, parsley, and lemon balm; and if you don't want that pesky mint to take over your garden, a planter is the perfect home for it. Use your porch trellis for growing pole beans, and plant zucchini where it can spread out its super-sized leaves and bright yellow blossoms to make a perfect ground cover. You will be greatly rewarded when you plant flats of mixed salad greens. If you have never eaten a salad made with just-picked greens, you will truly be amazed that you can really taste their freshness. Your local garden nursery will have flats of seeded plants that you can just put right in, so it couldn't be easier.

The best part of growing greens is harvesting, and the more you pick, the more they grow. There is nothing better than an early evening stroll in the garden and gathering up a couple of zucchini and peppers and adding them to whatever is on the grill. Slice them and toss with olive oil, salt, and a splash of balsamic vinegar and use as a bed for your grilled meat or fish. Dinner done! I can't think of anything more delicious—or healthier. Growing greens is not only a summer pleasure. Here in the Northeast Swiss chard, Brussels sprouts, and kale will still be producing right up until mid-November. Lucky me.

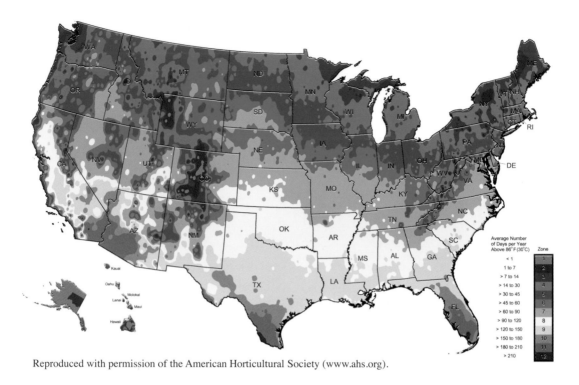

Average Number of Days per Year Above 86°F (30°C)	Zone
< 1	1
1 to 7	2
> 7 to 14	3
> 14 to 30	4
> 30 to 45	5
> 45 to 60	6
> 60 to 90	7
> 90 to 120	8
> 120 to 150	9
> 150 to 180	10
> 180 to 210	11
> 210	12

Reproduced with permission of the American Horticultural Society (www.ahs.org).

Find out what Heat Zone you live in to determine the number of days over 86 degrees your region experiences. Plants vary in their ability to withstand heat as well as frost. The U.S. Department of Agriculture's map (www.usna.usda.gov/Hardzone/ushzmap.html) will help you know the approximate length of time between the last and first frost for your area. You can add to this time by using a cold frame, which is basically a box with a transparent top that will trap radiant heat, which protects your plants from freezing, so that you can start plants sooner and harvest them later than otherwise.

I use raised beds, which are basically just a four-sided frame about a foot high resting on the ground. I fill them with about half earth and half composted manure. It gives you more control over your soil mix, and makes your garden easier to tend to. One of my friends has her beds raised on "legs" about three feet off the ground, which eliminates bending and protects her plants from creatures like rabbits and ground hogs. If you put your beds on legs, you can even store your garden tools and supplies underneath. My years of apartment living in New York have made me aware of using every inch of space. If you have the room, as I do, plant a thick hedge around your beds, like Mr. McGregor (Peter Rabbit's nemesis—or maybe that's vice versa). It is not foolproof, but it looks better than a fence, and it helps to steer critters in a different direction. You can add a

little more protection by putting chicken wire along the inside perimeter. The great thing about leafy greens is that they are prolific growers, so a little sacrifice for hungry animals is not such a bad thing, albeit annoying. They'll grow back, and when they do, sometimes I sprinkle cayenne pepper over everything, even along the bottom of the hedge and along the pathways. If you are bothered by deer, I'm sorry. You may have to pick up your greens at the local farmers' market. When considering your soil, it is good to determine the pH levels. Typically, you can have your soil tested at a local agricultural extension center. You can also find out the percent of organic matter, which is an indicator of the naturally available nitrogen that is released as the organic matter breaks down. This is about all you have to know to fertilize your garden soil properly. A nominal fee is charged for these services. After you receive the results of your soil, you will know which type of potting soil mixture to buy. The proportions of nitrogen, phosphorus, and potassium are typically designated by numbers such as 5-10-5, 12-12-12, or 6-24-24.

Phosphorus is the most important fertilizer for starting new plants and should be set where roots develop. Ammonium nitrate is important for asparagus, cabbage, broccoli, cucumber, peas, beans, peppers, spinach, kale, and mustard and turnip greens. Nitrogen comes from breaking down organic matter, yearly maintenance, and side dressings for particular circumstances. Leafy vegetables need it earlier than fruit-bearing plants, which do better if nitrogen is added when they start to flower.

Soils are either more sand or more clay. Organic matter is the third constituent and is very controllable and should be from 2 to 4 percent. This is achieved by adding animal manures and green manures, which are legumes that are folded under while still in the green stage. You can also use peat moss, leaf mold, and compost. Manure should be well rotted, applied in the fall, and folded under. Compost is made by gathering waste material, such as grass, leaves, and plant refuse in layers six to eight inches deep. The pile should not be more than five feet wide and five feet high. Add a little soil and a handful of fertilizer to each layer as you build it up. Keep the pile moist. It takes six months to a year to mature.

Spread the seeds of greens on the soil and keep them well watered. Kale, cabbage, and lettuce are more difficult to grow from seed, so pick up sprouted plants at your nursery. If you want to start seeds inside, you will need to put them under grow lights. Alternating rows of greens with onions and or marigolds will diminish your loss to insects. Be on the lookout for aphids and other tiny bugs that your guests may not appreciate.

My really big secret to gardening is: "Don't forget to water!" Watering in the morning is best so that rot and fungus are avoided. Nobody likes to go to bed with their feet wet, so avoid late evening watering. Check your soil—if it feels dry below two inches, it needs water. Moisture should extend downwards at least five inches. Look at your plants—if they look dry and stressed, water them immediately, and give them a real good soaking.

Check your plants regularly for pests of both the bug and disease varieties. A bit of discoloration is acceptable, but totally engulfed plants should be pulled and discarded. When you have questions, my best advice is to ask the nursery where you purchase your plants. Most are growing local, so they can give you the best information about growing in your area.

It's also a good idea to have a real gardener, or, at least, your friends, look at your plants for both fun and productivity. My idea of a garden party is a stroll along the garden beds with a glass of wine and a good friend. Pick up a couple of peppers and head for the grill.

There is truly nothing more rewarding or more delicious than growing your own greens, and I urge everyone to plant them, nourish them, and enjoy.

artichokes

Artichokes are edible thistles with Mediterranean origins. They were introduced to this country by Spanish settlers in California in the 1600s but didn't become widely grown until the 1920s. Today almost all commercially grown artichokes in the country come from Castroville, California, where Marilyn Monroe was crowned Artichoke Queen in 1948.

Their growing season is a long one, usually from October to June, and artichokes are at their peak and most plentiful from March to May. Look for fresh ones that are deep green, compact, and heavy with tightly packed leaves. Avoid those with leaves that are yellow and dry, or spread out. They can be stored, unwashed, in a plastic bag in the refrigerator for up to four days. Artichokes are usually served as a first course, boiled or steamed, with melted butter, aioli, or hollandaise sauce for dipping. They are also excellent in soups, salads, and savory side dishes.

Stuffed Artichokes

Stuffed artichokes are a fabulous first course, and the broth that you get from slowly baking them is delicious. Be sure to serve these with lots of crusty bread to savor every last drop.

makes 6 servings

6 large artichokes

2 lemons, halved

6 garlic cloves, chopped, divided

1 cup chopped fresh flat-leaf parsley

1 tablespoon kosher salt

2 cups fine dry breadcrumbs

1 cup freshly grated Parmesan cheese

4 tablespoons ($\frac{1}{2}$ stick) butter, melted

1 cup dry white wine

3 cups chicken or vegetable broth

2 tablespoons olive oil

1. Preheat the oven to 300°F.

2. Cut off the artichoke stems, cutting them flush with the bottom. Do not discard the stems. With a sharp knife, cut an X into the base of each artichoke. Slice off about 1 inch from the top of each artichoke and discard. Rub the cut ends with the lemon halves to prevent discoloring. With kitchen shears, snip the tops of each leaf to remove the thorny tips.

3. In the bowl of a food processor or blender, add 4 cloves of the chopped garlic, parsley, and salt and pulse until very fine. Transfer to a mixing bowl and mix with the breadcrumbs and Parmesan cheese. Pour the melted butter over all and mix well.

4. Gently pry open the artichoke leaves just to loosen a bit. Holding the stem end in the palm of your hand, pile on the stuffing, tapping lightly to fill between the leaves. Arrange the artichokes in a roasting pan stem side down so that they fit snugly in the pan. Pour in the wine, broth, the remaining 2 tablespoons chopped garlic, and enough water to reach about 1 inch up the side of the roasting pan.

5. Peel the reserved stems with a vegetable peeler and cut them into $\frac{1}{2}$-inch slices; add to the roasting pan. Drizzle the olive oil over all and cover the pan with a lid or aluminum foil. Put the pan in the oven and bake the artichokes for about 3 hours, or until a knife easily penetrates the stem end.

6. Remove from the oven, spoon a bit of the broth and some stem slices into six soup plates and top with the artichokes. The artichokes can be served hot or at room temperature, but the broth, which can be reheated, must be hot.

Steamed Artichokes with Dipping Sauces

This is another good way to serve artichokes: Prepare them as you would the stuffed artichokes, but omit the stuffing. Fill a roasting pan with three parts water and one part broth. Cover and bake for about three hours.

Here are three different dipping sauces for steamed artichokes. They are fantastic for serving with artichokes, individually or together.

Hollandaise Sauce

The trick to this sauce is cooking it very slowly so the yolks don't cook too quickly; otherwise the mixture will become lumpy.

> *makes 4 to 6 servings*
> 2 tablespoons fresh lemon juice
> 4 egg yolks
> 2 sticks (½ pound) unsalted butter, divided

Whisk together the lemon juice and egg yolks in a small saucepan. Add 1 stick of the butter and cook over medium heat, stirring until the butter is completely melted. Add the remaining stick of butter and stir constantly until the butter has melted and the sauce is thick. Serve in individual dipping bowls.

Artichokes are an excellent source of vitamin C, folate, and a significant source of magnesium and potassium.

A medium boiled artichoke provides:

calories	64
protein	3.5g
carbohydrate	14.3g
fiber	6.9g
fat	0.19g
vitamin C	15%
vitamin K	22%
folate	27%
niacin	7%
magnesium	13%
manganese	13%
potassium	10%
phosphorous	9%

Avocado-Lime Butter

Try this smooth and creamy dip with steamed artichokes as well as other steamed or raw vegetables.

makes 4 to 6 servings

2 avocados, peeled, pitted, and cut into chunks

1 stick (¼ pound) salted butter, softened

Juice of ½ lime

Dash of green Tabasco sauce

Put the avocados, butter, lime juice, and Tabasco sauce in a blender and process until creamy. Serve in individual dipping bowls.

Bagna Cauda

Bagna cauda originated from the Piedmont region of Northern Italy. The deep flavor of anchovies, garlic, and good olive oil make a perfect warm dipping sauce for steamed artichokes and crusty bread.

makes 4 to 6 servings

6 to 8 flat anchovies packed in oil

½ cup extra-virgin olive oil, divided

4 garlic cloves, finely minced

Hot pepper flakes

1 stick (¼ pound) unsalted butter

½ cup chopped fresh flat-leaf parsley

In a medium saucepan, heat the anchovies with 2 tablespoons of the olive oil until very hot, smashing the anchovies with the back of a wooden spoon until they have dissolved into the oil. Add the garlic and hot pepper flakes to taste and cook until the garlic begins to simmer but not brown. Add the butter, the remaining 6 tablespoons olive oil, and the parsley and cook until the butter has melted. Serve immediately in individual dipping bowls.

Sautéed Baby Artichokes and Potatoes

You will find baby artichokes at their peak in the springtime. Although it's a labor of love to slice and remove the choke, it's well worth the effort. This is a fantastic side dish for roasted leg of lamb or pork loin. Mmmmmm.

makes 4 to 6 servings
1 lemon, cut in half crosswise
$1^1/_2$ pounds small red potatoes
16 baby artichokes
$^1/_4$ cup olive oil
3 or 4 garlic cloves, minced
$^1/_4$ teaspoon red pepper flakes
1 to 2 cups vegetable broth
Kosher salt

1. Fill a large bowl with cold water and squeeze half the lemon into it.

2. Rinse the potatoes, cut into quarters, and set aside.

3. Remove and discard the tough outer leaves of the artichokes down to the light green leaves. Trim the bottoms and the sides where the outer leaves were removed and slice the artichokes in half lengthwise. If they seem large, cut them into quarters. (They should be about the same size as the quartered potatoes.) Remove any purple leaves with a small paring knife. Rinse the chokes in cold water, rub each cut side with the remaining lemon half, and transfer them to the bowl of lemon water.

4. Heat the oil over medium heat in a large pot. Add the garlic and red pepper flakes and sauté for 1 minute. Drain the artichokes. Add the artichokes and potatoes to the pot and stir together for about 2 minutes to evenly coat the vegetables with the olive oil. Add 1 cup of the broth and bring to a simmer. Cover and cook over low heat for about 30 minutes, until the potatoes are cooked but not mushy. Check the pot occasionally, adding more broth if necessary. Add salt to taste and transfer to a serving dish. Drizzle with a bit of olive oil and serve at once.

asparagus

What does the word *asparagus* mean? The word *asparg* has either Greek or Persian roots and means "sprout," which makes sense because it was one of the world's earliest harvestable fresh vegetables.

Although asparagus now appears in markets year-round, the best asparagus is available from early April until late June. When buying asparagus, the rule is the fresher the better, as with all vegetables. Look for spears with straight firm stalks, uniform green color, and compact pointed tips with a lavender tint. Ideally, asparagus should be prepared and eaten on the same day it is purchased. However, it can be wrapped and stored, unwashed and uncut, in a plastic bag in the refrigerator for three to four days.

Fresh asparagus is so elegant and can be cooked and served in a number of delicious ways. Try it in a salad with shiitake mushrooms or with celery and walnuts; steamed with garden-fresh chives and mint; in a lighter-than-air frittata; or roasted and stirred into a bold-flavored risotto.

Roasted Asparagus
and Shiitake Mushroom Salad

When asparagus is roasted it takes on a pungent, almost nutty flavor. And when it's combined with warm shiitake mushrooms the flavor is unbeatable. This salad is delicious as a first course or as a side with grilled pork, lamb, or steak.

makes 6 servings

3 tablespoons extra-virgin olive oil, divided

2 pounds asparagus, ends trimmed

Kosher salt

2 garlic cloves, thinly sliced

2 cups shiitake mushrooms, thinly sliced

1 tablespoon fresh lemon juice

Freshly ground black pepper

4 cups mixed salad greens

1. Preheat the oven to 350°F.

2. Brush a baking sheet with 1 tablespoon of the oil. Put the asparagus on the baking sheet, season to taste with salt, and toss to coat. Spread the asparagus in an even layer and roast until tender and lightly browned, 20 to 30 minutes.

3. Heat the remaining 2 tablespoons oil in a large skillet or sauté pan. Add the garlic and cook over medium heat until softened, about 2 minutes. Add the mushrooms, lemon juice, and salt and pepper to taste and cook until browned, 5 to 7 minutes. Remove from the heat.

4. Just before serving, add the roasted asparagus to the mushrooms and reheat over medium-high heat, tossing constantly, until heated through, 1 to 2 minutes. Taste and adjust the seasonings, if necessary.

5. Arrange the salad greens on a platter and spoon the asparagus mixture over them. Add a bit more lemon juice, if desired, and serve at once.

Asparagus, Tomato, and Pecan Salad

This salad, made with tender asparagus and garden-fresh cherry tomatoes, tastes great with garlicky Mustard-Dill Vinaigrette. We like to make a generous amount of the vinaigrette and keep it on hand to drizzle over grilled vegetables, roasted potatoes, and fresh salad greens.

makes 1 cup vinaigrette, 6 servings salad

mustard-dill vinaigrette:

1 garlic clove, sliced

$1/2$ small yellow onion, coarsely chopped

$1/4$ cup chopped fresh dill

1 tablespoon Dijon mustard

$1/4$ cup balsamic vinegar

1/3 cup water

$1/2$ cup safflower oil

Kosher salt and freshly ground black pepper

salad:

$2^{1}/_{2}$ to 3 pounds slender fresh asparagus

6 cups fresh mixed salad greens

1 cup cherry tomatoes, halved

$1/2$ cup pecan halves, lightly toasted

1. To make the vinaigrette, put the garlic, onion, dill, mustard, vinegar, water, oil, and salt and pepper to taste in a food processor fitted with a steel blade or a blender and blend until smooth. The vinaigrette will keep, covered, in the refrigerator for up to 1 week.

2. To make the salad, cut or break off the tough ends of the asparagus stalks and discard.

3. In a large saucepan or skillet, bring enough lightly salted water to cover the asparagus to a boil over high heat. Add the asparagus, reduce the heat to a simmer, and cook just until tender, 3 to 5 minutes. Drain well. Chill the asparagus for 1 hour.

4. In a serving bowl, toss the greens and tomatoes together with about $1/4$ cup of the vinaigrette. Toss the asparagus in a separate bowl with about 2 tablespoons of the vinaigrette, then place over the salad greens. Sprinkle with the toasted pecans and add a bit more vinaigrette, if desired. (You will have about $1/2$ cup of the vinaigrette left over.) Serve at once.

Asparagus, Celery, and Walnut Salad

Walnut oil has a delicate, nutty flavor and tastes wonderful in a salad of fresh asparagus and chopped celery. Be sure to use the freshest, crunchiest celery you can find.

makes 6 servings

salad:

2$^1/_2$ pounds slender fresh asparagus

3 celery ribs, cut into $^1/_4$-inch pieces on the diagonal

walnut dressing:

6 tablespoons walnut oil

2 tablespoons fresh lemon juice

2 tablespoons finely minced red onion

Kosher salt and freshly ground black pepper

3 tablespoons chopped walnuts

1. To make the salad, cut or break off the tough woody ends of the asparagus stalks and discard.

2. In a large saucepan or skillet, bring enough lightly salted water to cover the asparagus to a boil over high heat. Add the asparagus, reduce the heat to a simmer, and cook just until tender, 3 to 5 minutes. Drain well. Put the asparagus and celery in a shallow serving bowl or platter.

3. To make the dressing, whisk together the oil, lemon juice, onion, and salt and pepper to taste in a small bowl. Pour the dressing over the vegetables and toss lightly to coat. Marinate, covered, at room temperature for at least 1 hour.

4. Sprinkle the walnuts over the salad and serve.

Asparagus with Fresh Chives and Mint

Asparagus used to be a harbinger of spring, but today fresh green asparagus can be found in markets year-round, in varying levels of flavor. We still believe that the best time to indulge in fresh asparagus is from early April through the end of June. When buying asparagus look for straight stalks with tightly closed and pointed tips.

makes 6 servings

2 pounds slender fresh asparagus

4 tablespoons ($1/2$ stick) unsalted butter, divided

2 tablespoons finely chopped shallots

1 teaspoon finely grated lemon zest

1 tablespoon fresh lemon juice

1 teaspoon kosher salt

3 tablespoons finely snipped fresh chives

2 teaspoons finely chopped fresh mint leaves

Kosher salt and freshly ground black pepper

1. Cut or break off the tough woody ends of the asparagus stalks and discard. (Young asparagus may not have tough ends.)

2. In a large saucepan or skillet, bring enough lightly salted water to cover the asparagus to a boil over high heat. Add the asparagus, reduce the heat to simmer, and cook for 3 to 5 minutes, just until tender. Drain well.

3. In a saucepan, melt 1 tablespoon of the butter over medium heat. Add the shallots and sauté for 2 to 3 minutes until transparent and soft. Add the remaining 3 tablespoons butter and stir the shallots and butter until the butter melts. Remove from the heat and stir in the lemon zest, lemon juice, and salt. Stir in the chives and mint.

4. Transfer the asparagus to a shallow bowl and carefully toss with the melted butter. Season with salt and pepper to taste and serve at once.

Sautéed Asparagus, Peas, and Basil

Here's a fantastic combination of greens in terms of taste, texture, and looks. Although fresh peas are ideal for this dish, frozen ones will work well too.

makes 6 servings

1 tablespoon olive oil

1 tablespoon unsalted butter

¼ cup finely chopped shallots

1 pound fresh asparagus, trimmed and cut into 1-inch pieces

2½ cups shelled fresh peas (about 2 pounds),
  or 1 (10-ounce) package frozen peas, thawed

½ cup chopped fresh basil

Kosher salt and freshly ground black pepper

1. Heat the oil and butter in a large skillet over medium heat. Add the shallots and cook, stirring frequently, until just tender, about 3 minutes.

2. Stir in the asparagus and peas. Cover and cook, stirring occasionally, until the vegetables are just tender, about 10 minutes. Stir in the basil and add salt and pepper to taste and cook for another minute. Serve at once.

Asparagus has an exceptional balance of nutrients. It has more folic acid, which helps in blood cell production and prevention of liver disease, than any other vegetable. Asparagus contains cancer-fighting glutathione and also has rutin, which strengthens blood vessels. It is rich in the amino acid asparagine and very low in sodium.

One cup of asparagus has approximately:

calories	32
carbohydrates	3.5g
fat	0.8g

Of the recommended daily value, this portion provides:

vitamin C	73%
vitamin K	180%
vitamin E	11%
folate	61%
niacin	9%
magnesium	4%
manganese	13%
potassium	10%
phosphorous	9%
selenium	10%

Bella's Easter Asparagus

This recipe comes from Liz's sister's mother-in-law, Bella Buonocore. It was her tradition to gather all the girls in the family in the kitchen to help cook the Easter feast. She taught them to how to prepare this asparagus dish by carefully rolling the spears in the breadcrumb mixture like a rolling pin so it would stick well to the asparagus. This is a lovely accompaniment to roasted lamb or ham.

makes 6 servings
2 pounds thick asparagus, ends trimmed
1 cup flour
Kosher salt and freshly ground black pepper
2 eggs
4 cups fine breadcrumbs
1 cup freshly grated Parmesan cheese
2 garlic cloves, minced
$\frac{1}{2}$ cup finely chopped fresh flat-leaf parsley
$\frac{2}{3}$ cup canola oil, for frying
$\frac{1}{3}$ cup olive oil, for frying

1. Wash the asparagus and lay in a large pan with 1 cup of water. Bring to a boil and blanch for 3 minutes. Drain and rinse under cold water to prevent further cooking.

2. In a shallow bowl, mix together the flour and salt and pepper to taste. In another shallow bowl, whisk the eggs and 2 tablespoons of water together. In another bowl, combine the breadcrumbs, cheese, garlic, and parsley. Mix together until well blended and spread out on a baking sheet.

3. Roll 1 asparagus spear in the flour, then in the egg mixture, and then in the breadcrumb mixture until firmly packed with crumbs. Transfer to a sheet of waxed paper. Repeat with the remaining spears.

4. Heat the canola oil and olive oil in a large frying pan or skillet until hot but not smoking. Fry the asparagus until crispy and golden, about 3 minutes a side. Do not overcrowd the pan. Remove and drain on a wire rack or paper towels. Keep in a warm oven until all of the asparagus are fried. Serve hot.

Asparagus and Mushroom Frittata

We love making frittatas. They're terrific for breakfast or lunch, and they're equally good served hot, warm, or at room temperature. This one, made with fresh asparagus and mushrooms, is especially good.

makes 6 to 8 servings

8 eggs, at room temperature

$3/4$ cup freshly grated Gruyère cheese

$1/4$ cup minced fresh chives

Kosher salt and freshly ground black pepper

2 tablespoons unsalted butter

$1/2$ cup chopped shallots

12 ounces thin asparagus, ends trimmed
  and cut into 1-inch pieces (about 2 cups)

1 cup diced shiitake mushrooms

$1/4$ cup freshly grated Parmesan cheese

1. Preheat the oven to 350°F and grease a 9 x 12-inch baking pan or dish with butter.

2. In a large bowl, whisk together the eggs, Gruyère cheese, and chives until well combined. Add salt and pepper to taste and whisk again.

3. Heat the butter in a large skillet over medium heat. Add the shallots and sauté for 4 minutes. Add the asparagus and mushrooms and sauté until tender, about 8 minutes. Whisk into the egg mixture.

4. Pour the mixture into the prepared pan and sprinkle with the Parmesan cheese. Bake until the top of the frittata is firm and lightly browned, about 25 minutes. Serve hot, warm, or at room temperature.

Roasted Asparagus Risotto

Risotto is absolutely wonderful teamed with oven-roasted asparagus—it infuses the rice with big, bold flavor. When making this dish, be sure to stir the risotto constantly during cooking and be careful not to overcook the rice. This is a terrific dish to serve as an appetizer or a light supper for a change of pace from pasta.

makes 6 appetizer or 4 main course servings

2 pounds asparagus

1 tablespoon kosher salt

3 tablespoons olive oil, divided

2 cups vegetable broth

3 cups water

3 garlic cloves, minced

1$\frac{1}{2}$ cups Arborio rice

$\frac{1}{2}$ cup dry white wine

Kosher salt and freshly ground black pepper

1 tablespoon fresh lemon juice

$\frac{1}{2}$ cup chopped fresh flat-leaf parsley, for garnish

1. Preheat the oven to 325°F.

2. Rinse the asparagus and snap off the tough woody ends of the asparagus stalks and discard. Arrange in a single layer on a baking sheet with the water that is clinging to them. Sprinkle with the salt and 1 tablespoon of the olive oil and toss to coat. Bake for 15 minutes; toss the asparagus and bake for an additional 15 minutes until lightly browned. The time will vary depending on the thickness and freshness of the stalks. Remove from the oven and set aside.

3. Combine the broth and water in a large saucepan and bring to a very low simmer on the back burner of the stove. Heat the remaining 2 tablespoons olive oil in a heavy 2-quart pot over medium heat. Add the garlic and cook for 1 to 2 minutes, until golden but not brown. Add the rice and stir until it is well coated and has absorbed some of the flavored oil, about 2 minutes. Pour in the wine and bring to a simmer, stirring until it is almost fully absorbed. Slowly add the simmering broth to the rice, one ladleful at a time. Stir constantly to prevent the rice from sticking. As soon as one ladleful of broth has been absorbed by the rice, add another ladleful. If you think you may run out of liquid, add more water to the simmering broth. The entire process will take 15 to 20 minutes, and the rice should be tender but still firm. Taste for doneness, and when it seems nearly done, cut the asparagus into 1-inch lengths and stir into the rice. Add just a bit more broth, if necessary.

4. Spoon the risotto into large pasta bowls. Add salt and pepper to taste, sprinkle with lemon juice, and garnish with parsley. Serve at once.

beans

Green beans (also called string beans or snap beans) are from the legume family. They originated in South America and although they are said to be the most frequently consumed vegetable in the United States, they have only been raised commercially in this country since the mid-1800s.

They are available year-round and their peak season runs from May through October. When selecting green beans, look for beans that are sold loose so they can be hand picked. They should be crisp, blemish-free, and bright green in color. If you're growing green beans in your garden, plant them in a sunny location and when the soil is warm (at least 70°F). It's a good idea to stagger the plantings of green beans throughout the growing season to have a continuous supply of them. Green bean plants are the gift that keeps on giving—the more you pick, the more they will grow.

Green beans are so simple to prepare. They're wonderful in many ways, such as tossed with a bit of lemon juice and olive oil, added to a roasted potato salad, or slowly braised with tomatoes and onions—just to name a few.

Green Bean, Sweet Corn, and Olive Salad

This simple summery salad is perfect picnic or barbecue fare.

makes 6 servings

salad:

2 pounds fresh green beans, trimmed

3 ears fresh corn, husked

2 tablespoons finely chopped fresh basil

2 tablespoons finely chopped fresh flat-leaf parsley

Juice of $1/2$ lemon

vinaigrette:

$1/3$ cup extra-virgin olive oil

1 tablespoon balsamic vinegar

Dash of hot sauce

Kosher salt and freshly ground black pepper

$1/4$ cup pitted and halved kalamata olives

1. To make the salad, in a saucepan of boiling salted water, cook the beans until crisp-tender, 3 to 4 minutes. With a slotted spoon, transfer the beans to a colander and rinse under cold running water; drain. Transfer to a large bowl and set aside.

2. In the same saucepan of boiling water, cook the corn for 3 minutes; drain and cool. Scrape the kernels by holding the ears upright on a plate and scraping downward with a small sharp knife. Add the corn to the beans, along with the basil and parsley. Sprinkle with the lemon juice and toss.

3. To make the vinaigrette, in a small bowl, whisk together the oil, vinegar, and hot sauce and season with salt and pepper. Drizzle over the salad and toss thoroughly. Transfer to a serving platter or shallow bowl and top with the olive halves. Serve warm, chilled, or at room temperature.

Roasted Potato and Green Bean Salad

Who doesn't love potato salad? We make it all year—for summer barbecues, picnic lunches at the beach, autumn potluck dinners, and just about any other occasion. Here is one of our favorites that adds green beans to the spuds. Be sure to mix the vinaigrette with the potatoes and green beans while they are still warm.

makes 6 servings

salad:

2 pounds small red potatoes, halved or quartered

8 garlic cloves, peeled

3 tablespoons olive oil

Kosher salt

$3/4$ pound green beans, trimmed and cut into 1-inch pieces

Chopped fresh flat-leaf parsley, for garnish

vinaigrette:

1 teaspoon Dijon mustard

2 teaspoons horseradish

$1/2$ cup extra-virgin olive oil

1. Preheat the oven to 325°F.

2. To make the salad, place the potatoes and garlic on a baking sheet. Add the olive oil and salt to taste and toss well to coat. Roast for about $1^1/_2$ hours, until the potatoes are fork-tender, tossing them occasionally.

3. Shortly before the potatoes are finished, bring a pot of salted water to a boil. Add the beans and boil for 2 to 3 minutes; drain.

4. To make the vinaigrette, whisk the mustard and horseradish together in a small bowl. Slowly add the olive oil, whisking until emulsified.

5. Transfer the warm potatoes and beans to a large serving bowl. Pour the vinaigrette over and toss well. Taste and adjust the seasonings. Garnish with parsley and serve.

Green Bean, Prosciutto, and Parmesan Salad

This excellent salad has a great combination of colors, textures, and, of course, tastes.

makes 6 servings

1$\frac{1}{2}$ pounds fresh green beans, rinsed and trimmed

1 tablespoon Dijon mustard

$\frac{1}{2}$ tablespoon sherry vinegar

$\frac{1}{4}$ cup olive oil

Kosher salt and freshly ground black pepper

Fresh shaved Parmesan

2 cups torn radicchio leaves

6 thin slices prosciutto

Fresh shaved Parmesan cheese

1. In a saucepan of boiling salted water, cook the beans until crisp-tender, 4 to 5 minutes. Rinse under cold running water and drain. Transfer to a large bowl.

2. In a small bowl, whisk together the mustard and vinegar. Slowly add the olive oil in a steady stream, whisking constantly until emulsified. Add salt and pepper to taste and whisk again. Pour the vinaigrette over the beans and toss to coat.

3. Arrange the radicchio on a platter or divide among six salad plates. Spoon the beans over the radicchio. Cut each slice of prosciutto into thin 3-inch strips and arrange over the beans. Top with fresh shaved Parmesan. Add a bit of fresh cracked pepper, if desired, and serve.

Sautéed Green Beans
with Parmesan and Lemon

Here is one of those go-to side dishes that you will want to make again and again. You may want to try it with other cheeses such as Gruyère, Manchego, or Asiago.

makes 4 to 6 servings

1 pound green beans, rinsed and trimmed

1 tablespoon unsalted butter

3 tablespoons freshly grated Parmesan cheese

Kosher salt and freshly ground black pepper

1 tablespoon fresh lemon juice

1. Bring a pot of water to a boil and add the green beans. Boil for 1 to 2 minutes, depending on their freshness. Remove from the heat and rinse under cold water to retain color.

2. Heat the butter in a large sauté pan over medium-low heat. Add the beans and toss to coat. Cook slowly until they begin to brown, 2 to 3 minutes. Sprinkle with the cheese and toss quickly to coat evenly. Transfer the beans to a serving bowl. Add salt and pepper to taste and sprinkle with the lemon juice. Serve at once.

Stewed Beans and Sweet Onions

This recipe works beautifully with green beans that aren't perfectly fresh—it happens—or with larger, thick-skinned pole beans.

makes 4 to 6 servings
1 pound green beans or large pole beans
1 tablespoon unsalted butter
1 large Vidalia onion, thinly sliced
$\frac{1}{2}$ cup chicken or vegetable broth
Kosher salt and freshly ground black pepper

1. Rinse the beans and trim the ends. If they are large, remove the string that runs down the length of the bean with a paring knife. Cut into 1-inch pieces.

2. Heat the butter over low heat in a skillet or sauté pan with a lid. Add the onion and cook until soft and translucent, about 10 minutes, being careful not to burn. Add the beans and broth, cover, and cook for 15 minutes. Remove the lid, season to taste with salt and pepper, and cook to reduce the remaining liquid. Serve at once.

Sautéed Green Beans
with Tomatoes and Capers

Here's another recipe for slow-cooked green beans. The caramelized onions and juicy cherry tomatoes add a rich and meaty flavor to the beans. You can also make this dish with chopped black or green olives instead of capers.

makes 4 to 6 servings
1 pound green beans, rinsed and trimmed
1 tablespoon olive oil
½ red onion, thinly sliced
1 cup halved cherry tomatoes
Kosher salt and freshly ground black pepper
1 tablespoon capers

1. Bring a large pot of salted water to a boil. Add the beans, cook for 2 minutes, and drain.

2. Heat the olive oil over low heat in a skillet or sauté pan with a lid. Add the onion and cook over low heat until they begin to caramelize, 10 to 15 minutes. Add the tomatoes and their juices. Season with salt and pepper to taste and stir. Cover the pan and cook over very low heat, stirring occasionally, until the tomatoes are softened, about 20 minutes. Add the capers and cook for an additional 10 minutes. Serve at once.

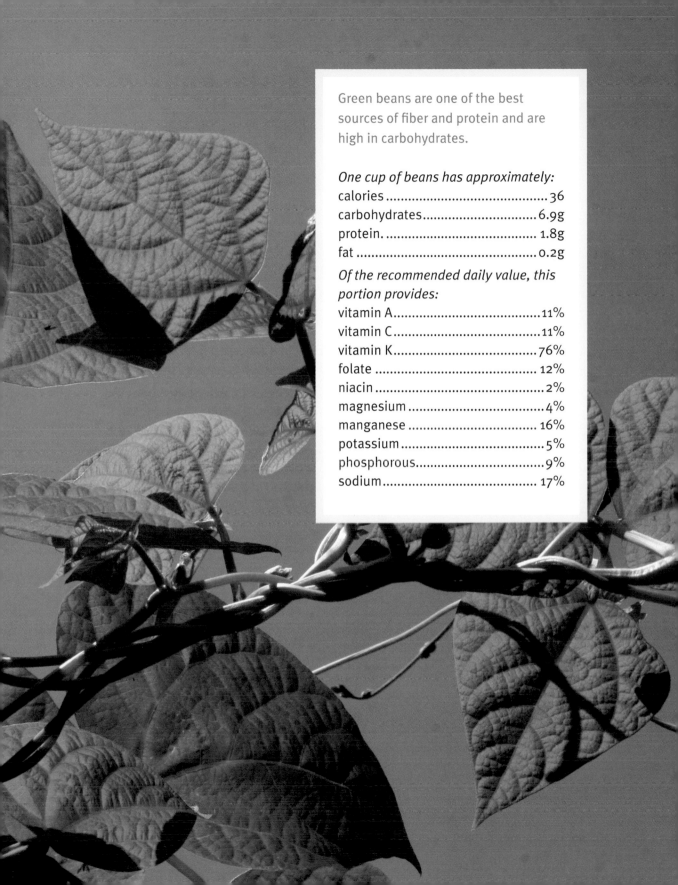

Green beans are one of the best sources of fiber and protein and are high in carbohydrates.

One cup of beans has approximately:

calories 36
carbohydrates 6.9g
protein. 1.8g
fat 0.2g

Of the recommended daily value, this portion provides:

vitamin A 11%
vitamin C 11%
vitamin K 76%
folate 12%
niacin 2%
magnesium 4%
manganese 16%
potassium 5%
phosphorous 9%
sodium 17%

Spicy Green Beans with Garlic and Ginger

These green beans have a great pickle taste, and they're terrific served chilled or at room temperature.

makes 4 to 6 servings
$1/2$ cup white vinegar
$1/2$ cup rice wine vinegar
1 cup water
2 garlic cloves, thinly sliced
2 quarter-size pieces of ginger, thinly sliced
1 pound green beans, rinsed and trimmed

1. Combine the vinegars, water, garlic, and ginger in a saucepan and bring to a boil. Reduce the heat to medium low and simmer until the liquid is reduced by half.

2. Put the beans in a steamer basket and steam, or cook them in boiling water for 2 to 3 minutes. Drain and rinse under cold water. Transfer the beans to a shallow nonreactive baking dish or casserole and pour the vinegar mixture over them. Toss to coat, cover loosely with foil, and marinate at room temperature for at least 6 hours, tossing occasionally. Serve at room temperature or chill in the refrigerator. The beans can be made up to three days ahead of time and stored in the refrigerator.

Lemon-Grilled Chicken and Green Beans

Charcoal-grilled chicken and fresh green beans pair beautifully in this wonderful main-course dish. You can substitute olive oil for walnut oil, if necessary.

makes 6 servings

Juice of 2 lemons

Juice of 2 limes

2 garlic cloves, thinly sliced

$1/4$ cup olive oil

3 whole chicken breasts
  (about $41/2$ pounds), split

2 pounds fresh green beans,
  trimmed

1 tablespoon white wine vinegar

1 teaspoon fresh lemon juice

$1/2$ cup walnut oil

$1/2$ cup walnut halves, toasted

Kosher salt and freshly ground black pepper

$1/2$ cup chopped fresh flat-leaf parsley,
  for garnish

1. Combine the lemon juice, lime juice, and garlic in a medium bowl. Slowly whisk in the olive oil to combine. Place the chicken in a large nonreactive baking dish. Pour the marinade over the chicken, turning the chicken to coat. Cover and marinate in the refrigerator, turning occasionally, for up to 8 hours or overnight.

2. Prepare a medium-hot gas or charcoal grill (coals are covered with a light coating of ash and glow deep red), or preheat the broiler. Remove the chicken from the marinade, reserving the marinade. Grill or broil the chicken 6 to 9 inches from the heat, turning occasionally, until nicely browned and the juices run clear when the chicken is pierced with a fork, about 30 minutes. Baste the chicken often with the reserved marinade during the first 20 minutes of grilling.

3. Remove the chicken from the heat and set aside to cool. When cool enough to handle, remove the meat from the bones and tear into $11/2$-inch pieces. Transfer to a large bowl.

4. In a saucepan of boiling salted water, cook the beans until crisp-tender, 4 to 5 minutes. Rinse under cold running water and drain. Add the beans to the chicken and toss gently.

5. In a small bowl whisk together the vinegar and lemon juice. Slowly add the walnut oil in a steady stream, whisking constantly until emulsified.

6. Drizzle about $1/3$ cup of the vinaigrette over the chicken and beans and toss to coat. Heap the salad onto a platter or individual salad plates and sprinkle with the walnut halves. Drizzle with the remaining vinaigrette and season to taste with salt and pepper. Garnish with parsley and serve at once.

beets and beet greens

It is a historical fact that beets were once prized for their leaves, or tops, instead of their better-known crimson bulbs. We love both parts of the beet and they taste wonderful together.

Beets are available year-round and are at their best when picked fresh between late June and early October. When selecting beets look for smooth, dark red skins and, most importantly, crisp green leaves. Pass up any beets that have yellowing or brownish leaves. Before storing beets trim the greens, leaving an inch or two at the top of the beets. They can be stored, unwashed, in an open plastic bag in the refrigerator for up to two weeks. The greens can be stored, unwashed, in a plastic bag for two or three days.

Beet greens are a favorite green of ours. They have a deep and pungent flavor that pairs well with roasted or steamed beets and tangy vinaigrette or a touch of butter and lemon. Young beet leaves also make a tasty addition to a salad of mixed greens.

Beet Greens and Beets with Balsamic Vinaigrette

This dish of warm beets and beet greens flavored with a piquant vinaigrette is a wonderful cold-weather alternative to a salad. When buying beets, always look for those topped with fresh-looking beet greens.

makes 6 servings

2 bunches (about 2 pounds) beets with greens

2 tablespoons vegetable oil

2 tablespoons balsamic vinegar

2 tablespoons fresh lemon juice

6 tablespoons extra-virgin olive oil

Kosher salt and freshly ground black pepper

1. Cut the beet greens from the beets, discarding any wilted or dried greens, and trim the stems. Rinse, dry, and set the greens aside.

2. Peel and quarter the beets; then cut them into $1/4$-inch-thick slices. Put them in a steamer over boiling water, cover, and cook over medium-high heat until just tender, 15 to 20 minutes.

3. Heat the vegetable oil in a skillet over medium-high heat. Sauté the beet greens until wilted, about 3 minutes. Put them in a serving dish, set aside, and keep warm.

4. Whisk the vinegar and lemon juice together in a small bowl. Whisk in the olive oil and season to taste with salt and pepper.

5. To serve, spoon the warm steamed beets over the beet greens. Drizzle with the vinaigrette and serve at once.

Beet juice lowers blood pressure by dissolving calcium deposits from arteries. Beets have betaine, which inhibits colon and stomach cancer.

One cup of boiled beet greens has approximately:

calories	39
carbohydrates	7.9g
protein	3.7g
fat	0.3g

Of the recommended daily value, this portion provides:

vitamin A	220%
vitamin C	60%
vitamin E	13%
vitamin K	871%
vitamin B6	10%
thiamin	11%
riboflavin	24%
niacin	4%
folate	5%
niacin	4%
calcium	16%
iron	15%
magnesium	24%
manganese	37%
potassium	37%
phosphorous	6%
sodium	14%

Beet Greens and Beets with Maple Walnuts

Here's a fantastic way to serve beet greens and beets. It makes a great side dish for poultry, especially roast duck. When preparing the beets before boiling, leave a bit of stem on them. They'll bleed less in the water.

makes 4 servings
1 bunch (about 1 pound) beets with greens
1 tablespoon balsamic vinegar
2 tablespoons unsalted butter, divided
1 tablespoon maple syrup
$1/2$ cup chopped walnuts

1. Cut the greens off the top of the beets, leaving about $1/2$-inch of stem on the beets, and rinse. Bring a large pot of water to a boil, add the beets, and cook until fork-tender, 40 to 50 minutes. Drain in a colander and rinse with cold water until they are cool enough to handle. Rub the skin and the tops off with your fingers under cold running water. This is called "slippin' the beets."

2. Cut the beets into thin wedges and transfer to a bowl. Toss them with the vinegar and set aside. (This can be done several hours ahead of time. Warm the beets on the stove or in a microwave oven before serving.)

3. Rinse the beet greens and coarsely chop. Melt 1 tablespoon of the butter in a sauté pan and add the greens. Cover and simmer gently over medium heat for about 10 minutes. Pile the greens onto a platter and top with the beets.

4. Melt the remaining 1 tablespoon butter in a small saucepan over medium heat. Add the maple syrup and walnuts and stir constantly until the mixture is thick and syrupy, being careful that it doesn't burn. Pour over the beets and greens and serve at once.

bok choy

Although bok choy is technically classified as a cabbage, it bears little resemblance to the round green or red cabbages that we are familiar with. It has long been a staple of Asian cooking and is becoming increasingly popular and widely available in this country because of its sweet, peppery flavor and slightly crunchy texture. Baby bok choy is a smaller variety of bok choy; it is a bit more tender and sweeter and it cooks faster.

When selecting bok choy look for firm stalks and healthy, dark green leaves. Bok choy can be stored in the refrigerator for up to five days after rinsing and drying it and putting it in an open plastic bag.

Bok choy is an excellent stir-fry dish to accompany poultry and seafood dishes. It's also good stirred into soups and chopped and added to salads.

Bok Choy and Shiitake Mushroom Stir-Fry

Bok choy pairs very nicely with shiitake mushrooms. Baby bok choy is more tender than regular bok choy, but both work well in this recipe. Because bok choy cooks quickly, be sure to have all your ingredients ready before starting this stir-fry.

makes 4 to 6 servings

$1/2$ cup chicken broth

2 tablespoons Asian fish sauce (nam pla)

1 teaspoon soy sauce

2 tablespoons canola oil

2 garlic cloves, thinly sliced

2 tablespoons minced fresh ginger

1 cup stemmed, thinly sliced shiitake mushrooms

3 pounds bok choy or baby bok choy (leaves and stems),
   cut into 1-inch pieces

1. In a small bowl, whisk together the broth, fish sauce, and soy sauce; set aside.

2. In a large skillet or wok, heat the oil over high heat until very hot. Add the garlic and ginger and stir-fry for about 30 seconds, until fragrant. Add the mushrooms and stir-fry for 2 minutes. Add the bok choy and stir-fry until crisp-tender, about 3 minutes.

3. Add the broth mixture and cook until the bok choy is tender but still bright green and the sauce is slightly reduced, about 3 minutes longer. Serve immediately.

Baby Bok Choy with Black Bean Sauce

Fermented black beans, also known as salted black beans, are available in Asian markets. They add a rich, deep flavor to this lovely bok choy dish. This works well as a side or a vegetarian main dish served over rice.

makes 4 to 6 servings

2 tablespoons fermented black beans

2 garlic cloves, minced

1 tablespoon rice wine vinegar

1 tablespoon soy sauce

1 teaspoon sugar

3 pounds baby bok choy, rinsed and dried

1 tablespoon sesame oil

3/4 cup chicken broth, vegetable broth, or water, divided

1 teaspoon cornstarch

1. Rinse the black beans thoroughly in cool water and drain. Put them in a small bowl with the garlic, vinegar, soy sauce, and sugar. Mash the mixture with the back of a fork until it is well incorporated and becomes a paste.

2. Trim the bottom ends of the bok choy without detaching the leaves.

3. Heat the sesame oil in a wok, add the black bean paste, and stir until heated through. Add the bok choy and toss well. Add 1/2 cup of the broth or water, cover, and cook over low heat until tender, about 3 minutes. Transfer the bok choy to a large serving bowl and keep warm. Mix the cornstarch in the remaining 1/4 cup broth and add to the wok. When the sauce thickens, pour it over the bok choy and serve at once.

Bok Choy and Pork Stir-Fry

This is a great dish to serve with rice or soba noodles for supper. We make it with thin slices of pork, but it's also good with chicken. Look for nam pla in Asian markets or in the international section of the supermarket.

makes 4 servings

2 tablespoons Asian fish sauce (nam pla)

1 tablespoon low-sodium soy sauce

1 small chili pepper, stemmed, seeded, and minced,
  or red pepper flakes to taste

2 teaspoons sugar

1 teaspoon fresh lime juice

1 medium head bok choy (1 to 1$\frac{1}{2}$ pounds), rinsed and dried

2 tablespoons grapeseed or safflower oil

3 garlic cloves, thinly sliced

1$\frac{1}{2}$ cups thinly sliced cooked pork

1. In a small bowl, whisk together the fish sauce, soy sauce, chili pepper, sugar, and lime juice. Set aside.

2. Cut the bok choy stems into 1-inch pieces and roughly chop the leaves. Heat the oil in a large skillet over medium-high heat. Add the garlic and cook for 1 minute. Turn the heat up, add the bok choy stems, and cook, stirring and shaking the pan, until they are slightly tender, about 3 minutes. Add the bok choy leaves and cook for 1 minute.

3. Add the pork to the skillet and pour the sauce over the pork and bok choy. Cook, stirring and shaking the pan, for 2 to 3 minutes. Serve at once.

Bok choy contains indoles, a nitrogen compound which, with its fiber, lowers cancer risk. Bok choy has more beta-carotene than other cabbages.

One cup of boiled bok choy has approximately:

calories	20
carbohydrates	3.1g
protein	2.7g
fat	0.3g

Of the recommended daily value, this portion provides:

vitamin A	144%
vitamin C	74%
vitamin E	1%
vitamin K	72%
vitamin B6	14%
folate	17%
niacin	4%
calcium	16%
iron	10%
magnesium	5%
manganese	12%
potassium	5%
phosphorous	5%
sodium	2%

broccoli

Broccoli is a member of the *brassica oleracea* family, whose members also include cauliflower, cabbage, collards, and Brussels sprouts. Its name comes from the Italian word *brocco,* meaning "sprout" or "shoot," which comes from the Latin word *brachium,* which means "arm" or "branch."

Though broccoli is widely available year-round, its peak season is from October to April. When buying broccoli, look for compact crowns that have tightly closed heads and that are dark green or bluish green in color. Avoid any heads that are yellowish and stalks that are limp. It's important to keep broccoli cold if not using right away. It will keep, unwashed and wrapped in a plastic bag, in the refrigerator for up to three days.

There are many ways to prepare this healthy, delicious, and versatile vegetable, from crudités with dip to elegant soups to hearty salads or side dishes.

Broccoli, Leek, and Apple Soup

Tart Granny Smith apples add a nice bite to this smooth, luxurious soup.

makes 4 to 6 servings

2 tablespoons unsalted butter

1 onion, thinly sliced

2 leeks (white and green parts), rinsed, trimmed, and diced

2 Granny Smith apples

1 bunch broccoli, trimmed and cut into small dice (about 3$\frac{1}{2}$ cups)

3$\frac{1}{2}$ cups chicken or vegetable broth

1 russet potato, peeled and diced

$\frac{1}{2}$ teaspoon celery seeds

Pinch of cayenne pepper

Kosher salt and freshly ground black pepper

Fresh chives, for garnish

1. Melt the butter in a large soup pot over low heat. Add the onion and leeks, cover, and cook for 5 minutes, stirring occasionally. Peel and core 1 of the apples and cut into small dice. Add to the pan and cook, covered, for 10 minutes.

2. Add the broccoli and broth. Increase the heat to medium and bring to a boil. Reduce the heat to low, cover, and cook for 15 minutes, stirring occasionally. Add the potatoes, celery seeds, cayenne, and salt and pepper to taste. Cover and simmer until the potatoes are fork-tender, about 15 minutes. Remove from the heat and set aside to let cool.

3. Transfer the soup to a blender or food processor and blend until smooth. This will have to be done in batches. Taste and adjust the seasoning, if necessary. (The soup can be made ahead of time and will keep, covered, in the refrigerator for a day.)

4. Reheat the soup. Cut the remaining apple into small pieces or thin strips. Spoon the soup into soup bowls and garnish each serving with the apples and chives and serve at once.

Broccoli with Sesame Oil Sauce

In this recipe, broccoli florets and stems are lightly steamed and tossed together with a vinaigrette made with sesame oil, rice vinegar, and soy sauce. This side dish is delicious served warm, cold, or at room temperature.

makes 4 servings
1 large bunch broccoli
$1/4$ cup toasted sesame oil
$1/4$ cup rice vinegar or sake
1 tablespoon low-sodium soy sauce
Pinch of sugar
Pinch of red pepper flakes
Toasted sesame seeds, for garnish

1. Separate the broccoli into small florets. Peel the stalks and cut them on the diagonal into $1/2$-inch pieces.

2. Steam the broccoli over simmering water until crisp-tender, 6 to 8 minutes. Remove from the heat and drain. Transfer the broccoli to a shallow serving bowl.

3. In a small bowl, whisk together the oil, vinegar, soy sauce, sugar, and red pepper flakes until well combined. Taste and adjust the seasonings, if necessary. Pour the vinaigrette over the broccoli and toss lightly to coat.

4. Just before serving, sprinkle the broccoli with sesame seeds and serve warm or at room temperature. The broccoli can also be chilled for a few hours before serving.

Crunchy Broccoli Slaw

Make this fantastic summery slaw in the morning and let it marinate in the refrigerator all day. Serve it with grilled chicken, pork, or fish for dinner that night.

makes 6 servings
$1/2$ cup cider vinegar
$1/2$ cup golden raisins
4 large broccoli crowns, rinsed
2 carrots, shredded
1 cup walnuts, roughly chopped
2 tablespoons mayonnaise
Kosher salt and freshly ground black pepper

1. Heat the vinegar in a small saucepan until it begins to boil. Remove from heat, add the raisins, and let stand until cool and the raisins are plump, about 20 minutes.

2. Cut the broccoli into chunks and put in food processor. Process until finely chopped. Transfer to a large bowl and add the shredded carrots and walnuts. Stir in the raisins and vinegar. Add the mayonnaise and mix well. Add salt and pepper to taste. Chill in the refrigerator for up to 8 hours.

Warm Broccolini and Potatoes

Although it is sometimes referred to as baby broccoli, broccolini is actually a hybrid of broccoli and Chinese chard. It can be used like conventional broccoli, but it requires less cooking time and it turns bright green when it is steamed or sautéed. The whole plant is edible, including the stems. It tastes great in this robust dish with red potatoes.

makes 6 servings

$1^1/_2$ pounds small red potatoes, scrubbed

1 pound broccolini, trimmed, heads cut into flowerets

1 garlic clove, minced

2 tablespoons cider vinegar

1 teaspoon Dijon mustard

$^1/_4$ cup olive oil

$^1/_2$ teaspoon paprika

Kosher salt and freshly ground black pepper

2 scallions, thinly sliced

$^1/_4$ cup chopped fresh flat-leaf parsley

1. Put the potatoes in a large pot and cover with cold water. Bring to a boil and cook until tender, about 20 minutes. Drain, cool, and cut into quarters.

2. Steam the broccolini over boiling water until just tender, 3 to 5 minutes.

3. While the potatoes and broccolini are cooking, whisk the garlic, vinegar, and mustard together in a small bowl. Slowly add the olive oil, whisking until emulsified. Add the paprika and salt and pepper to taste and whisk again.

4. Put the warm potatoes and broccolini in a large bowl. Add the scallions, parsley, and vinaigrette to the bowl and toss well. Taste and adjust the seasonings, if necessary, and serve.

The two major types of broccoli are those which are grown for heads of flowers, and those which are grown for heads of flowers and their leaves.

Broccoli contains phytochemicals and is one of the foods that is most likely to prevent colon cancer. Broccoli minimizes the risk of cataracts and protects blood vessels.

One large stalk of boiled broccoli has approximately:
calories 98
carbohydrates............................ 20.1g
protein 6.7g
fat 1.1g

Of the recommended daily value, this portion provides:
vitamin A..87%
vitamin C......................................303%
vitamin E..20%

vitamin K...................................494%
vitamin B6....................................28%
folate 76%
niacin 8%
pantothenic acid 17%
calcium 11%
iron 10%
magnesium 15%
manganese 27%
potassium.....................................23%
phosphorous................................19%
sodium...31%

broccoli rabe

Broccoli rabe, also known as *broccoli raab, broccoli di rape,* and *rapini,* is a fantastic green with origins in the Mediterranean and China. It was introduced to this country by Italian farmers in the 1920s. Even though its name comes from the Italian phrase broccoletti di rape, meaning "little stalks of turnip," it is a matter of debate whether it is a member of the broccoli or the turnip family.

When selecting broccoli rabe look for firm, dark green stems with compact heads. Florets should be tightly closed, not open or yellow. It can be stored in the refrigerator in a plastic bag for up to three days.

It is best to steam or blanch broccoli rabe for about three minutes before sautéing it to remove its natural bitterness. Flavorful ingredients such as garlic, onions, chilies, sausages, and Parmesan cheese are excellent with broccoli rabe as they stand up to and enhance its delicious, pungent bite.

Braised Broccoli Rabe and Red Onions

Although broccoli rabe is usually cooked as a quick sauté, it also is very tasty when slowly braised with sweet caramelized red onions.

makes 4 servings
2 tablespoons olive oil
1 large red onion, thinly sliced
1 large bunch (about 1 pound) broccoli rabe, stems and tough outer leaves trimmed
2 to 3 tablespoons chicken broth or water
Kosher salt and freshly ground black pepper

1. Heat the oil in a large sauté pan over low heat. Add the onion and cook until very soft and caramelized, 15 to 20 minutes.

2. Add the broccoli rabe and cook, tossing occasionally, for about 5 minutes. Add the broth or water, cover and cook until softened, about 15 minutes. Add more liquid if the rabe seems too dry. Add salt and pepper to taste, toss again, and serve at once.

Broccoli rabe is low in saturated fat and a good source of pantothenic acid. Broccoli rabe is also a good source of dietary fiber.

One bunch of cooked broccoli rabe has approximately:
calories 144
carbohydrates............................. 14.9g
protein 16.7g
fat 2.3g

Of the recommended daily value, this portion provides:
vitamin A..................................396%
vitamin C....................................270%
vitamin E.......................................55%
vitamin K..................................1398%

vitamin B6......................................48%
folate 78%
niacin...44%
pantothenic acid 20%
calcium 52%
iron 31%
magnesium...................................29%
manganese 83%
potassium.....................................43%
phosphorous.................................36%
copper..16%
selenium 8%
sodium...10%

Broccoli Rabe with Sausage

Bitter broccoli rabe and spicy Italian sausage are an unbeatable combination. We like to serve this in bowls with chunks of toasted bread to mop up the tasty broth. Or for a heartier main dish, spoon it over warm penne or farfalle.

makes 6 servings

2 bunches (about 2 pounds) broccoli rabe

3 tablespoons olive oil

1 pound Italian sausage

4 garlic cloves, thinly sliced

1 cup chicken or vegetable broth

Kosher salt and freshly ground black pepper

1. Cut off about $1/2$ inch of the stalk ends of the broccoli rabe and discard. Holding the bunch together, roughly slice the rabe crosswise 3 or 4 times including leaves, so you have chunks about 3 inches long. Rinse under cold water in a colander and set aside.

2. In a large sauté pan with 2-inch sides and a lid, heat the olive oil over medium heat. Remove the sausage from the casings, if necessary, and cook, breaking it up with a spatula.

3. When the sausage is browned, add the garlic and cook, stirring constantly, for 1 minute. Add the broth and stir, scraping up all the sausage bits from the pan. Bring to a simmer and add the rabe. Toss with tongs to incorporate the broth and oil. The pan will be very full but the rabe will cook down quickly.

4. Cover the pan, and simmer over low heat for about 25 minutes, tossing occasionally. If you prefer a crunchier texture, turn off the heat after 15 minutes and let it sit for 5 minutes. Add salt and pepper to taste and serve at once.

If you are lucky enough to have leftover Broccoli Rabe with Sausage, it is spectacular when reheated. We like to use it to make a beautuful frittata for breakfast or brunch. Butter a 9 x 12 shallow casserole, and beat 7 eggs. Give the rabe and sausage a rough chop, and add it to the eggs along with a cup of grated cheese like cheddar or Monterey Jack, or whatever you have on hand that melts well. Mix all together and pour into the pan. Bake at 350°F for 30 minutes, which will give you just enough time to change out of your pajamas. Your guests will think you are magical.

Broccoli Rabe
with Hot Chili and Soy Sauce

Here's a quick-sautéed broccoli rabe with a tasty Asian accent. It's very good served hot from the pan or served chilled as a side salad. Look for hot chili-flavored oil in Asian markets or the international section of the supermarket.

makes 4 to 6 servings

2 tablespoons canola or safflower oil

3 shallots, thinly sliced

3 garlic cloves, thinly sliced

1 large bunch (about 1 pound) broccoli rabe,
  stems and tough outer leaves trimmed

1 tablespoon sake

1 tablespoon hot chili-flavored oil

2 tablespoons soy sauce

1. Heat the oil in a large sauté pan or wok over medium heat. Add the shallots and garlic and cook until softened, about 5 minutes.

2. Add the broccoli rabe and cook over medium-high heat, tossing with tongs, for 1 minute. Whisk together the sake, oil, and soy sauce and pour over the broccoli rabe. Cook the broccoli rabe, tossing occasionally, until it is wilted and the sauce is absorbed, 6 to 8 minutes. Drizzle with some additional chili oil and serve at once.

Note: To serve cold, chill the broccoli rabe in the refrigerator for at least 2 hours.

brussels sprouts

Brussels sprouts are members of the cruciferous vegetable *brassica olerica* family. They were first cultivated in Belgium in the 1500s and were introduced to this country in the 1800s.

They are a fall crop, and some think that they are at their best and have a sweeter taste after the first frost of the season. When selecting Brussels sprouts look for those with the smallest and tightest buds. They should be bright green and crisp to the touch. Avoid any that have loose or yellowing leaves. Wrapped in plastic, they can be stored in the refrigerator for up to three days.

When preparing Brussels sprouts be careful not to overcook them or they will have a strong sulfurous flavor and odor, which is the reason they often get a bad rap. But when they are quickly sautéed or gently roasted, they develop a mildly nutty flavor and they taste quite wonderful.

Sautéed Brussels Sprouts, Carrots, and Apples

The key to this tasty slaw-like dish is to cook everything quickly and to be sure that you use cider vinegar for a nice tangy finish. Brussels sprouts and carrots can be easily shredded in a food processor.

makes 4 to 6 servings
2 tablespoons olive oil
6 shallots, thinly sliced
10 ounces Brussels sprouts, trimmed and shredded
3 carrots, peeled, trimmed, and shredded
1 apple, unpeeled and finely chopped
2 tablespoons cider vinegar
Kosher salt and freshly ground black pepper

1. Heat the olive oil in a large skillet over medium heat. Add the shallots and cook, stirring often, for 5 minutes. Add the Brussels sprouts and carrots and cook, stirring, for 5 minutes.

2. Add the apple and cook, stirring, for 5 minutes. Add the vinegar and salt and pepper to taste and cook, stirring, for 2 minutes. Serve at once or cover and refrigerate for a few hours and serve cold.

Sautéed Brussels Sprouts
with Bacon and Walnuts

The subtle flavor of Brussels sprouts is a perfect partner for rich and salty bacon in this dish. Since it cooks quickly on top of the stove and needs no reheating, it's a good side to serve for Thanksgiving.

makes 6 servings

4 cups (about 1 pound) Brussels sprouts, trimmed

1 cup chicken broth

2 slices thick-cut bacon

1 tablespoon olive oil

2 garlic cloves, thinly sliced

4 shallots, trimmed and thinly sliced

2 tablespoons finely chopped walnuts

1. Bring a saucepan of water to a boil. Add the Brussels sprouts and cook for 3 minutes. Drain and cool. Cut in half and set aside. Meanwhile, heat the broth in a small saucepan over medium heat. Reduce to $1/4$ cup, about 10 minutes, and set aside.

2. Heat a large skillet over medium heat. Add the bacon and cook until browned, about 5 minutes. Drain on paper towels and crumble.

3. Pour off all but 1 tablespoon of the bacon drippings. Add the olive oil and heat over medium heat. Add the garlic and shallots and cook, stirring often, for 5 minutes. Add the Brussels sprouts and cook, stirring until coated, for 2 to 3 minutes. Add the reduced broth and cook, stirring, for 5 minutes. Add the bacon and walnuts and cook, stirring, for 5 minutes. Serve at once.

Roasted Brussels Sprouts, Parsnips, and Carrots

This dish of roasted sprouts and root vegetables is an excellent accompaniment to roast chicken or pork. Toasted pecans add a good crunchy finish.

makes 4 to 6 servings

10 ounces Brussels sprouts, trimmed and halved

6 carrots, peeled and cut on the diagonal into 1-inch pieces

4 parsnips, peeled and cut on the diagonal into $1/2$-inch pieces

3 tablespoons olive oil

Kosher salt and freshly ground black pepper

$1/4$ cup pecans, toasted and chopped

1 tablespoon fresh lemon juice

2 tablespoons chopped fresh flat-leaf parsley

1. Preheat the oven to 375°F.

2. Put the Brussels sprouts, carrots, and parsnips in a large roasting pan. Add the olive oil and salt and pepper to taste and toss well to coat. Roast, stirring occasionally, until the vegetables are fork-tender, 45 to 50 minutes. Transfer to a serving bowl or platter.

3. Sprinkle the pecans, lemon juice, and parsley over the vegetables. Serve at once.

Brussels sprouts reduce the risk of cancer and its crucifers support cardiovascular health. They also help to decrease triglycerides, cholesterol esters, and birth defects.

Brussels sprouts can be enjoyed all winter long as they are a cold-hardy vegetable. The colder the weather, the better they taste. Most people who say they don't like Brussels sprouts have never eaten a fresh properly cooked one. A sprout should be fork-tender but not mushy, and should retain most of its green color.

One boiled Brussels sprout has approximately:
calories 8
carbohydrates............................. 1.4g
protein 0.5g
fat 0.1g

Of the recommended daily value, this portion provides:
vitamin A..3%
vitamin B1 .... 1%
vitamin B2...................................... 1%
vitamin C......................................22%
folate 3%
niacin 1%
pantothenic acid 1%
calcium 1%
iron 1%
magnesium 1%
potassium 2%
phosphorus 1%

cabbage

Cabbage is a truly international vegetable. The Irish, English, French, Russian, and Hungarian people are among the many who consider it an important part of their culinary heritages.

The word "cabbage" is derived from the French word *caboche,* which means "head." It is presumed to have originated in the Mediterranean region of Europe and was introduced to America in the mid-1500s.

Most varieties of cabbage are available in markets year-round. Look for those with compact, heavy heads that have a generous amount of leaves. Also check the bottom to make sure that the leaves are not separated from the stem. Fresh, uncut cabbage can be stored, unwashed, in a plastic bag for up to two weeks.

Cabbage can be prepared in so many delectable ways. It adds a delicious depth and sweetness to soups; it is the fresh and crunchy star of slaws and salads; and when it is sautéed or stir-fried, it makes a wonderful savory side dish. It's no wonder that everyone loves this versatile vegetable.

Cabbage, White Bean, and Kielbasa Soup

This flavorful soup, made with cabbage and vegetables, white beans, and topped with kielbasa is a fantastic bowl of comfort food.

makes 6 servings

2 tablespoons olive oil

3 garlic cloves, thinly sliced

1 red onion, coarsely chopped

4 celery ribs, coarsely chopped

4 carrots, peeled and coarsely chopped

1 cup chopped fresh flat-leaf parsley, divided

Kosher salt and freshly ground black pepper

6 fresh or canned plum tomatoes, coarsely chopped, with their juices

$1/2$ pound green cabbage, shredded

4 cups chicken, beef, or vegetable broth

1 can (15.5 ounces) cannellini beans, drained and rinsed

$1/2$ to $3/4$ pound turkey kielbasa or chicken sausage

Freshly grated Parmesan cheese, for serving

1. Heat the oil over medium heat in a large soup pot or Dutch oven. Add the garlic, onion, celery, carrots, $1/2$ cup of the parsley, and salt and pepper to taste. Reduce the heat and cook, partially covered, stirring occasionally, until the vegetables are softened and caramelized, 20 to 25 minutes.

2. Add the tomatoes and their juices, cabbage, broth, and 2 cups of water. Mix well and simmer, partially covered, for 20 minutes. (The soup may be cooked up to this point and refrigerated until just before serving.)

3. About 15 minutes before serving, add the beans and cook over low heat, stirring occasionally. Taste and adjust the seasonings, if necessary.

4. Meanwhile, cook the kielbasa in a broiler or sauté in a skillet until lightly browned. Set aside and drain. When cool enough to handle, cut into $1/4$-inch rounds.

5. Ladle the soup into bowls, scatter the sausage over each serving, garnish with the remaining parsley, and serve with Parmesan cheese.

Creamy Cabbage Slaw

We like to use Chinese or napa cabbage in coleslaw. It has a light, delicate flavor that blends well with all of the other ingredients in this dish.

makes 6 to 8 servings

slaw:

$1/2$ head green cabbage, finely shredded

$1/2$ head Chinese or napa cabbage, finely shredded

2 carrots, finely shredded

Kosher salt and freshly ground black pepper

dressing:

$3/4$ cup mayonnaise

1 teaspoon Dijon mustard

$1^1/2$ teaspoons sugar

1 tablespoon white vinegar

$1/2$ teaspoon celery seeds

$1/2$ teaspoon paprika

1. To make the slaw, put the cabbages and carrots in a large bowl. Add salt and pepper to taste and toss well to combine.

2. To make the dressing, in a medium bowl, stir together the mayonnaise, mustard, sugar, vinegar, celery seeds, and paprika until well combined. Pour the dressing over the cabbage mixture and toss gently to combine. Season to taste with salt and pepper. Cover and chill the slaw until ready to serve.

3. Taste and adjust the seasonings, if necessary, and serve.

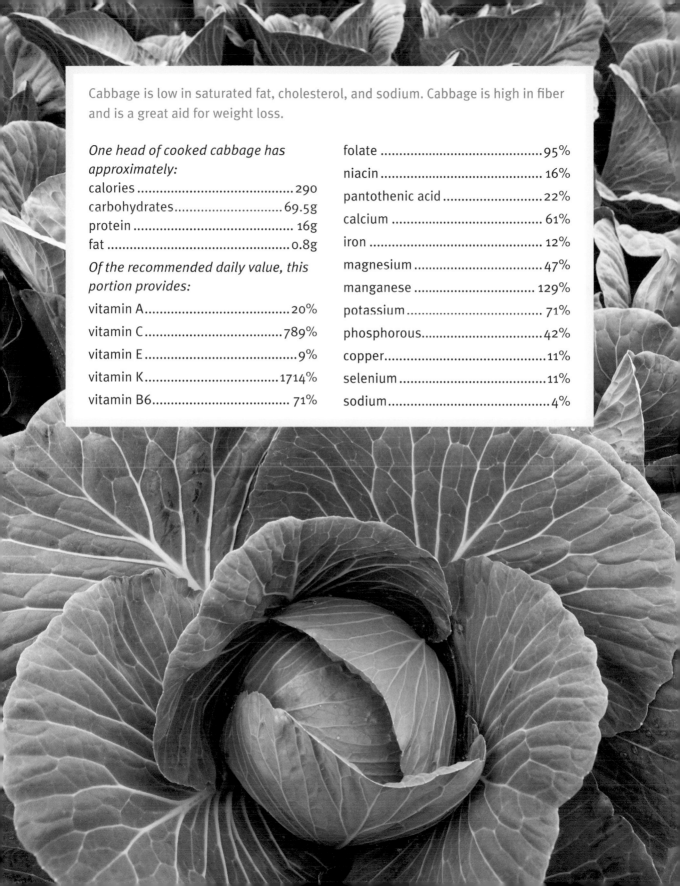

Cabbage is low in saturated fat, cholesterol, and sodium. Cabbage is high in fiber and is a great aid for weight loss.

One head of cooked cabbage has approximately:

calories 290
carbohydrates............................. 69.5g
protein 16g
fat 0.8g

Of the recommended daily value, this portion provides:

vitamin A.......................................20%
vitamin C....................................789%
vitamin E...9%
vitamin K...................................1714%
vitamin B6................................... 71%

folate 95%
niacin 16%
pantothenic acid 22%
calcium 61%
iron 12%
magnesium 47%
manganese 129%
potassium 71%
phosphorous................................42%
copper...11%
selenium 11%
sodium...4%

Savoy Cabbage, Radicchio, and Apple Slaw

This tangy slaw is quick and simple to prepare and is spectacular in presentation. The savoy cabbage has a delicate taste and texture that pairs well with slightly bitter radicchio.

makes 6 to 8 servings

$1/2$ head savoy cabbage, finely shredded

$1/2$ head radicchio, finely shredded

$1/2$ red onion, thinly sliced

1 Granny Smith apple, cut into 1-inch pieces

1 teaspoon rice vinegar

$1/4$ cup orange juice

$1/4$ cup mayonnaise

Kosher salt and freshly ground black pepper

1. Put the cabbage, radicchio, onion, and apple in a large bowl and toss together.

2. In a small bowl, whisk together the vinegar and orange juice. Add the mayonnaise and salt and pepper to taste and whisk until well combined. Pour over the cabbage mixture and toss until well coated.

3. Taste and adjust the seasonings, if necessary, and serve. The slaw will keep, covered, in the refrigerator for up to a day.

Stir-Fried Coleslaw

Warm stir-fried coleslaw is a terrific cabbage dish that pairs well with barbecued chicken or ribs.

makes 6 to 8 servings
6 cups shredded green cabbage
1 teaspoon kosher salt

stir-fry sauce:
2 tablespoons light soy sauce
2 tablespoons sugar
3 tablespoons rice wine vinegar
Pinch of red pepper flakes

2 tablespoons corn oil
2 tablespoons minced fresh ginger
1 medium red bell pepper, seeded, deveined, and thinly sliced
1 medium yellow bell pepper, seeded, deveined, and thinly sliced
2½ cups shredded carrots (about 4 carrots)
2 tablespoons sake
2 tablespoons minced scallions, for garnish

1. Put the cabbage in a large bowl and sprinkle with the salt. Let stand for 30 minutes.

2. Meanwhile, make the stir-fry sauce. Whisk together the soy sauce, sugar, vinegar, and red pepper flakes in a small bowl. Set aside.

3. Drain the cabbage and pat dry.

4. Heat the oil over high heat in a large skillet. Add the ginger and stir-fry for about 10 seconds. Add the bell peppers and toss for about 2 minutes. Add the cabbage and carrots and toss for another 2 minutes. Add the sake, cover, reduce the heat to medium, and cook until the vegetables are tender, about 2 minutes. Add the stir-fry sauce and stir-fry for 1 minute.

5. Transfer to a serving bowl or platter, garnish with the scallions, and serve.

Green Cabbage and Apple Bake

The sweet and savory flavors of apples and cabbage are a winning combination in this delicious side dish. It is excellent with a pork roast or ham.

makes 6 servings

1 head of cabbage

4 tablespoons (¹/₂ stick) unsalted butter, divided

¹/₂ cup apple cider

2 Granny Smith apples, quartered and cut into ¹/₄-inch slices

3 tablespoons brown sugar

¹/₂ cup dry unseasoned breadcrumbs

3 tablespoons brown sugar

1. Grease a 9 x 12-inch baking dish with butter and set aside. Cut the cabbage in half and remove the core. Cut each half into 4 wedges.

2. In a large pan with a lid, melt 2 tablespoons of the butter over medium heat. Add the cabbage and toss to coat. Pour in the cider, cover, and simmer for 10 minutes. Add the apple slices to the pan. Cover and simmer for 10 minutes longer. Transfer the mixture with its liquid to the prepared baking dish.

3. In a small bowl, combine the breadcrumbs and brown sugar. Melt the remaining 2 tablespoons butter and stir into the breadcrumbs and brown sugar. Sprinkle the mixture over the cabbage. Bake until the topping is golden brown and bubbly, about 20 minutes. Serve at once.

celery

Celery is believed to have originated in the Mediterranean, and the word "celery" comes from the French *céleri*. It was introduced to this country by European colonists in the 1800s.

It is available throughout the year and is at its best during the summer months, when it is in season. Look for celery with tight heads with compact outer stalks. It should look crisp and its leaves should be pale to bright green in color. Store it wrapped in a plastic bag in the refrigerator for up to two weeks.

Although some think of it as a rather ordinary vegetable, fresh celery, with its delicate flavor and crispy, crunchy texture is really fantastic. It's terrific to eat raw; it's a wonderful addition to soups and all types of salads; it tastes great when braised or stirred into stews and risottos; and it is essential in a Bloody Mary.

Celery Salad with Baby Arugula and Parmesan

This cool, fresh salad is a wonderful first course for a light fish or pasta dish, and it is yet another reason to grow lots of arugula in your garden.

makes 6 servings

12 large celery ribs, washed and trimmed
Kosher salt
$1/3$ cup olive oil
Juice of 1 lemon
6 cups baby arugula
$1/2$ cup freshly shaved Parmesan cheese, for garnish
Freshly ground black pepper

1. Slice the celery on the diagonal into $1/8$-inch pieces. Put in a large bowl and season generously with salt to taste.

2. Whisk together the olive oil and lemon juice and pour over the celery. Let the celery marinate for 1 to 2 hours, tossing often.

3. Arrange the arugula on a platter and spoon the celery mixture, including all of the dressing, evenly over the greens. Sprinkle the shaved Parmesan evenly over the salad and finish with a few grindings of black pepper.

Celery, Fennel, and Radish Salad

The delicate flavors of celery and fennel contrast nicely with crunchy radishes and salty ricotta salata cheese in this cool, refreshing salad.

makes 6 servings

1 fennel bulb, trimmed and julienned

4 celery ribs, trimmed and cut
  on the diagonal into 1/2-inch pieces

1 teaspoon red wine vinegar

1 teaspoon Dijon mustard

1 tablespoon fresh lemon juice

1 garlic clove, minced

1 tablespoon chopped fresh tarragon,
  or 1 teaspoon dried

1/4 cup extra-virgin olive oil

4 radishes, trimmed and sliced very thin

Kosher salt and freshly ground black pepper

1/4 pound ricotta salata cheese,
  cut into 1/4-inch slices

1. Put the fennel and celery in a large bowl. Whisk together the vinegar, mustard, lemon juice, garlic, and tarragon in a small bowl. Slowly add the olive oil and whisk until emulsified. Pour half of the vinaigrette over the salad and toss to coat. Add the radishes and salt and pepper to taste and toss again.

2. Drizzle a bit of the remaining vinaigrette over the salad and sprinkle the cheese over the top. Drizzle with a bit more vinaigrette and add more fresh pepper, if desired. Serve chilled or at room temperature.

Celery and Radicchio Risotto

Celery and shallots make an excellent base for this elegant risotto.

makes 4 main course or 6 appetizer servings

3 slices bacon

2$\frac{1}{2}$ cups chicken broth

1 tablespoon olive oil

2 shallots, thinly sliced

1 garlic clove, thinly sliced

$\frac{3}{4}$ cup chopped celery

1$\frac{1}{2}$ cups Arborio rice

1 cup dry red wine

Kosher salt

1 cup chopped radicchio leaves

1 tablespoon unsalted butter, at room temperature

$\frac{1}{4}$ cup freshly grated Parmesan cheese, plus more for serving

1. Fry the bacon until crisp. Drain on paper towels. When cool enough to handle, crumble and set aside.

2. Heat the broth until simmering in a saucepan. In a large sauté pan, heat the olive oil over medium heat. Add the shallots, garlic, and celery and sauté until softened, about 5 minutes.

3. Turn up the heat a bit and add the rice. Cook, stirring constantly, until the rice is well coated and translucent.

4. Add the wine and stir constantly. Once the wine has been absorbed by the rice, add the first ladle of broth and salt to taste. Reduce the heat to a simmer so the rice doesn't cook too quickly. Keep adding the broth, 1 ladleful at a time, allowing each addition to be absorbed before adding the next and stirring often, until the rice is soft but still has a bite, 15 to 20 minutes longer. Stir in the radicchio and reserved bacon.

5. Remove from the heat and add the butter and Parmesan cheese. Stir gently to combine. Cover the pan and let sit for 2 to 3 minutes. Serve in shallow soup bowls with additional Parmesan cheese.

Celery is believed to burn more calories than it provides while being a great source of dietary fiber. Celery is a good source of phalides and coumarins and is traditionally thought of as relieving bladder, kidney, and joint disease.

One serving (110g) of raw celery has approximately:

calories	18
carbohydrates	3.8g
protein	0.8g
fat	0.2g

Of the recommended daily value, this portion provides:

vitamin A	10%
vitamin C	6%
vitamin E	1%
vitamin K	40%
vitamin B6	4%
folate	10%
niacin	2%
pantothenic acid	3%
calcium	4%
iron	1%
magnesium	3%
manganese	6%
potassium	8%
phosphorous	3%
copper	2%
selenium	1%
sodium	4%

celery root

Celery root, also known as celery knob or celeriac, is a flavorful root vegetable that enjoys great popularity in Europe but is still a bit underappreciated here.

It originated in the Mediterranean and was eventually cultivated throughout Europe. It appeared in the U.S. in the early nineteenth century.

Celery root is available year-round but is at its best in winter through early spring. When selecting celery root, choose firm, medium-size roots that are heavy. Avoid any that have soft spots and a lot of rootlets and that feel spongy. To store them, trim and discard the stalk, and wrap the roots in plastic. They will keep in the refrigerator for up to one week.

This gnarly, bulbous root has an earthy aroma and an exquisite flavor that tastes like a combination of celery and parsley. It's delicious in soups, served raw in salads and slaws, and roasted or mashed with potatoes and other root vegetables.

Céleri Rémoulade

Like country paté, onion soup, and crème caramel, céleri rémoulade is a classic French bistro dish. It's an excellent side dish with any type of meat or fish—or serve with cooked, chilled green beans, cherry tomatoes, and niçoise olives for an impressive appetizer plate.

makes 6 servings

2 tablespoons fresh lemon juice

2 tablespoons Dijon mustard

$1/_2$ cup crème fraîche

$1/_4$ cup heavy cream

Kosher salt and freshly ground black pepper

1 celery root (about 1 pound)

$1/_2$ cup chopped fresh flat-leaf parsley

1. In a large bowl, whisk together the lemon juice, mustard, crème fraîche, cream, and salt and pepper to taste.

2. Trim the celery root, cut into quarters, and peel. Grate it in a food processor. Add the grated celery root to the mustard sauce and toss to coat. Add the parsley and toss again. Taste and adjust the seasonings, if necessary. Serve at once or chill for a few hours before serving.

Celery root is low in calories, high in dietary fiber, helps to regulate the absorption of nutrients, and suppresses hunger pangs. Celeriac is thought to aid in the healing of wounds.

One cup of cooked celeriac has approximately:

calories 42

carbohydrates................................. 9.1g

protein 1.5g

fat 0.3g

Of the recommended daily value, this portion provides:

vitamin C 9%

vitamin B6....................................... 8%

niacin 3%

calcium 4%

iron 4%

magnesium 5%

manganese 7%

potassium.. 8%

phosphorous.................................... 10%

copper.. 30%

selenium 1%

sodium... 4%

Celery Root and Cabbage Slaw

This is a good dish for a summer barbecue or picnic. Preparing celery root for this slaw is fairly easy—just cut off the ends, peel the bulb, and shred it finely in a food processor.

makes 6 to 8 servings

1 celery root (about 1 pound), trimmed, peeled,
  and finely shredded (about 3 cups)

½ small head green cabbage, thinly sliced (about 2 cups)

2 carrots, peeled and finely shredded (about 2 cups)

½ cup finely chopped fresh flat-leaf parsley

2 tablespoons fresh lemon juice

Salt and freshly ground black pepper

2 tablespoons Dijon mustard

2 tablespoons mayonnaise

2 tablespoons cider vinegar

¾ cup safflower or canola oil

¼ teaspoon ground paprika

Flat-leaf parsley sprigs, for garnish

1. Put the celery root, cabbage, carrots, and parsley in a large bowl. Sprinkle with lemon juice and season generously with salt and pepper. Toss well.

2. In a small bowl, mix the mustard and mayonnaise together. Stir in the vinegar, and when incorporated, whisk the oil into the mixture until the dressing is creamy and thick and all of the oil has been emulsified.

3. Pour the dressing over the vegetables and toss well. Add the paprika and toss again. Taste and adjust the seasonings, if necessary. Serve chilled or at room temperature and garnished with parsley sprigs. If you refrigerate the slaw for several hours, you may want to refresh it with a sprinkling of lemon juice before serving.

collard greens

Collard greens are members of the cabbage family *(brassica oleracea)* and their name is derived from *colewort,* the Anglo-Saxon term for "cabbage plants." It is thought that they originated in the Mediterranean region and also in China. Collard greens were introduced to this country by British colonists who settled in the South in the 1600s.

They are available year-round but many people think that they taste sweeter and better when harvested in cold weather. Look for collard greens that are deep green and plump, and avoid any that have yellow, brown, or wilted leaves. They will keep, unwashed, in a plastic bag in the refrigerator for up to four or five days.

Collard greens are a staple of southern cooking where they are often slow cooked with salted meats like ham hocks or smoked pork. They are also very good to stir into soups and casseroles and to sauté with a variety of other greens for a classic "mess o' greens" dish.

Smoky Collard Greens

Deep-flavored collard greens pair beautifully with smoked pork or turkey in this dish. Serve them with mashed white or sweet potatoes for a warm and soulful dinner.

makes 4 main course or 6 side dish servings
4 slices thick-cut bacon, cut into 1-inch pieces
2 shallots, roughly chopped
$1/2$ pound smoked meat, such as smoked pork or smoked turkey legs
1 large bunch collard greens, rinsed
Kosher salt

1. In a large heavy-bottomed soup pot, add the bacon and cook until the fat has been rendered. Remove and drain on paper towels. Add the shallots and cook until just translucent. Add the smoked meat and toss to coat. Add 2 quarts of water to the pot and bring to a boil.

2. Remove the center stems of the greens and discard. Coarsely chop the greens and add to the pot. Simmer, uncovered, for 50 to 60 minutes, adding more water if too dry. Remove the smoked meat and, when cool enough to handle, cut into small pieces and set aside.

3. Transfer the greens to a shallow serving bowl, reserving about 2 cups of the broth. Spoon the sliced meat over the greens and sprinkle with the reserved bacon. Taste the broth and add salt to taste, if necessary. Spoon the reserved broth over the greens and serve at once.

Collard greens are good sources of vitamin C and soluble fiber and contain multiple nutrients with potent anti-cancer properties, such as diindolylmethane and sulforaphane. Collard greens speed the liver's ability to render ingested toxins harmless.

One cup of boiled collards has approximately:

calories	49
carbohydrates	9.3g
protein	4g
fat	0.7g

Of the recommended daily value, this portion provides:

vitamin A	308%
vitamin C	58%
vitamin E	8%
vitamin K	1045%
vitamin B6	12%
folate	44%
niacin	5%
pantothenic acid	4%
calcium	61%
iron	27%
magnesium	10%
manganese	41%
potassium	6%
phosphorous	6%
copper	4%
selenium	1%
sodium	1%

Collard Greens and Parmesan-Roasted Fennel

This recipe is adapted from our friend, Philip Hoffman, a savvy New York City restaurateur and excellent home cook. The slow-roasted fennel adds a rich and creamy flavor to the greens, and if you have any leftovers, they should be added to homemade vegetable or tomato soup.

makes 6 to 8 servings

2 fennel bulbs

5 tablespoons olive oil, divided

Kosher salt and freshly ground black pepper

$1/2$ cup freshly grated Parmesan cheese, divided,
   plus more for serving

2 garlic cloves, minced

$1/2$ cup dry white wine

2 bunches (about 3 pounds) collard greens, rinsed, stemmed,
   and cut into 1-inch strips

2 tablespoons red wine vinegar

Red pepper flakes (optional)

1. Preheat the oven to 375°F. Brush a baking sheet with 1 tablespoon of the olive oil.

2. Cut the stems and fronds off the fennel and discard. Cut the bulbs in half lengthwise and remove the small interior core. Arrange the fennel halves, cut side down, on the baking sheet. Add salt and pepper to taste and drizzle with 2 tablespoons of the olive oil. Sprinkle with $1/4$ cup of the cheese. Bake until well caramelized, about $1^1/2$ hours. The cheese will form a crust on top of the fennel. Remove from the oven and let cool. With a sharp knife, coarsely chop the fennel and transfer to a bowl.

3. Heat the remaining 2 tablespoons olive oil in a large sauté pan over medium heat. Add the garlic and sauté until golden, about 3 minutes. Add the fennel and sauté for about 2 minutes. Add the wine and cook, stirring, for 1 minute. Add the collards and cook, tossing occasionally, until the collards start to wilt, about 5 minutes.

4. Add the vinegar, the remaining $1/4$ cup cheese, and the red pepper flakes, if using, and cook, tossing constantly, for 3 to 5 minutes. The greens should be wilted but not mushy. Taste and adjust the seasonings, if necessary. Garnish with additional cheese and serve at once.

cucumbers

Cucumbers are members of the gourd family and are technically classified as a fruit because they have an enclosed seed and develop from a flower. They originated in India and have been cultivated in this country since the mid-sixteenth century.

Cucumbers are available year-round but they are at their best and freshest in the summer, their prime growing season. Although there are many varieties of cucumbers the most common types are slicing cucumbers and pickling cucumbers. Choose ones that are firm and medium to dark green in color. Pass on any that are yellowish or have sunken water-soaked spots. They should be stored in the refrigerator for no more than three days, and they should never be left out at room temperature.

Cool and refreshing cucumbers are fabulous to eat raw with a sprinkling of sea salt or mixed with yogurt and fresh herbs to make a cool soup, raita, or tzatziki sauce. And they always add a sprightly crunch to all types of salads. Very cool, indeed.

Chilled Cucumber Soup with Yogurt and Dill

Cucumbers taste best in the summer, particularly if they are home grown or bought from a local farmer. Here they are cooked in a soup then chilled and served with yogurt and fresh dill.

makes 6 servings

3½ pounds cucumbers (5 to 6 medium),
   peeled, seeded, and chopped

1 small onion, sliced

3 tablespoons cider vinegar

3 tablespoons coarsely chopped fresh dill

8 to 9 cups chicken stock, preferably homemade

½ cup heavy cream or milk

Salt and freshly ground white pepper

1 to 1½ cups plain yogurt

Chopped fresh dill, for garnish

1 cucumber, thinly sliced, for garnish

1. In a stockpot, combine the cucumbers, onion, vinegar, and dill. Add the stock and bring to a boil, stirring, over high heat. Reduce the heat to medium-low and simmer, partially covered, for about 30 minutes, until the cucumbers are very soft. Set aside to cool until barely warm.

2. Purée the soup in a food processor fitted with a metal blade or a blender. (If using a blender, do this in batches.) Transfer to a bowl and stir in the cream. Season to taste with salt and pepper. Cover and chill for at least 4 hours or overnight.

3. Spoon about 2 tablespoons of the yogurt into each of six shallow, chilled soup bowls. Adjust the seasonings in the soup and then ladle over the yogurt. Garnish with dill and cucumber slices and serve.

Cucumbers soothe the skin, eyes, stomach, and urinary tract.
Cucumbers assist hair growth and fingernail toughness.

One-half cup of raw cucumber
with skin has approximately:
calories 8
carbohydrates............................... 1.9g
protein 0.3g
fat 0.1g

Of the recommended daily value,
this portion provides:
vitamin A... 1%
vitamin C...2%

vitamin K..11%
vitamin B6....................................... 1%
folate 1%
pantothenic acid 1%
calcium 1%
iron 1%
magnesium 2%
manganese 2%
potassium.......................................2%
phosphorous................................... 1%
copper.. 1%

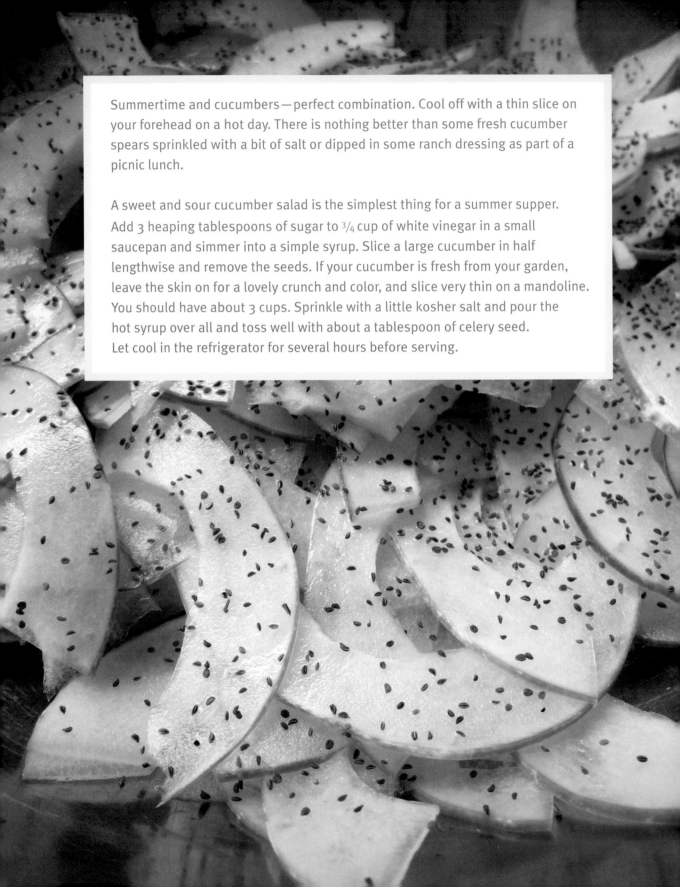

Summertime and cucumbers—perfect combination. Cool off with a thin slice on your forehead on a hot day. There is nothing better than some fresh cucumber spears sprinkled with a bit of salt or dipped in some ranch dressing as part of a picnic lunch.

A sweet and sour cucumber salad is the simplest thing for a summer supper. Add 3 heaping tablespoons of sugar to ¾ cup of white vinegar in a small saucepan and simmer into a simple syrup. Slice a large cucumber in half lengthwise and remove the seeds. If your cucumber is fresh from your garden, leave the skin on for a lovely crunch and color, and slice very thin on a mandoline. You should have about 3 cups. Sprinkle with a little kosher salt and pour the hot syrup over all and toss well with about a tablespoon of celery seed. Let cool in the refrigerator for several hours before serving.

Cucumber-Mint Raita

Raita, a yogurt-based Indian dish, is a staple in our kitchens. We use it as a salad, side dish, or condiment. Its light and creamy coolness complements very spicy dishes, and it is very refreshing. You can add other things like shredded carrots, scallions, and fresh basil to it too.

makes 6 servings

2 cups low-fat plain yogurt

1 teaspoon ground cumin

Pinch of crushed red pepper flakes

Pinch of sugar

Kosher salt and freshly ground black pepper

3 large cucumbers or 8 small Kirby cucumbers, peeled, seeded, and diced

1/2 red onion, finely diced

1/2 cup chopped fresh mint

1. Put the yogurt in a strainer lined with cheesecloth or a paper towel over a bowl. Drain for 15 minutes and then transfer to a medium bowl. Add the cumin, red pepper flakes, sugar, and salt and pepper to taste and whisk together until creamy and well combined.

2. Put the cucumbers, onion, and mint in a large bowl and toss together. Pour the yogurt mixture over them and toss well to combine. Taste and adjust the seasonings. Cover and chill the raita for a few hours before serving.

Cucumber and Shrimp Salad

This crunchy salad is just the thing to eat on a hot summer's day or night as a refreshing starter or main course. Use Greek yogurt in this recipe for extra creaminess.

makes 4 main course or 6 appetizer servings
1 pound large shrimp
2 large cucumbers, peeled, seeded, and cut into 1-inch dice
Kosher salt
2 celery ribs, trimmed and cut into 1-inch pieces
$\frac{1}{2}$ small red onion, thinly sliced
$\frac{1}{4}$ cup mayonnaise
$\frac{1}{4}$ cup plain yogurt
1 tablespoon white vinegar
3 tablespoons chopped fresh dill, divided
Freshly ground black pepper
$\frac{1}{2}$ bunch watercress, for serving

1. Bring a large pot of salted water to a boil. Add the shrimp and cook until they turn pink and rise to the top of the pot, about 4 minutes. Drain the shrimp, run under cool water, and peel. Chill in the refrigerator for an hour.

2. Meanwhile, put the cucumbers in a colander, sprinkle with salt, and let drain for 30 minutes. Transfer to a large bowl and add the celery and onion.

3. In a small bowl, mix the mayonnaise, yogurt, and vinegar together. Fold into the cucumber mixture and gently toss together. Add the shrimp, 2 tablespoons of the dill, and the pepper to taste and toss again. Taste and adjust the seasonings, if necessary. The salad can be made ahead of time and will keep, covered, in the refrigerator, for up to 4 hours.

4. To serve, arrange the watercress on a large platter or individual salad plates. Spoon the cucumbers and shrimp over the watercress and garnish with the remaining tablespoon of dill.

dandelion greens

Although many people think of the dandelion as a weed that grows wild in their lawns, fresh dandelion leaves are wonderful, edible greens. The word dandelion comes from the French *dent de lion* ("lion's tooth"), referring to the jagged edges of the plant's leaves. Dandelion greens originated in the Mediterranean and Asia where they were used for medicinal purposes as well as for eating. They were introduced to the United States by settlers from Europe in the 1600s.

The best time to pick dandelion greens is in early spring before their flowers bloom and they become tough. They should be eaten soon after picking.

Dandelion greens are a wonderful addition to soups, salads, and frittatas. And they are particularly good when quickly sautéed with a bit of butter and olive oil and other tasty ingredients. Don't overlook this delicious green that literally grows in your own backyard.

Sautéed Dandelion Greens with Smoked Ham

This quick-cooking dish of fresh dandelions and smoky ham is marvelous. Like all greens, their tangy flavor pairs well with the salty, smoky taste of ham or bacon.

makes 4 to 6 servings

1½ pounds dandelion greens, well rinsed

1 tablespoon olive oil

1 tablespoon unsalted butter

1 onion, finely chopped

3 garlic cloves, thinly sliced

2 tablespoons finely chopped smoked ham

Freshly ground black pepper

1. Separate the leaves and the stems of the greens. Chop the stems and set aside.

2. Heat the oil and butter in a large sauté pan or skillet over medium heat. Add the onion and cook for 1 minute. Add the garlic and cook, stirring occasionally, until golden, about 5 minutes. Add the ham and the dandelion stems. Cover and cook for 3 minutes.

3. Add the dandelion leaves, cover, and cook until the leaves start to wilt, about 1 minute. Remove the cover and raise the heat to high. Cook, tossing constantly, until the leaves are tender. Add pepper to taste and serve at once.

Dandelion greens are the traditional tonic of spring for cleansing the liver and kidneys. Dandelion greens are also an excellent source of vitamin K, which is proven to aid in weight loss when ingested.

One cup of boiled dandelion greens has approximately:

calories	35
carbohydrates	6.7g
protein	2.1g
fat	0.6g

Of the recommended daily value, this portion provides:

vitamin A	144%
vitamin C	32%
vitamin E	13%
vitamin K	724%
vitamin B6	8%
folate	3%
niacin	3%
pantothenic acid	1%
calcium	15%
iron	10%
magnesium	6%
manganese	12%
potassium	7%
phosphorous	4%
copper	6%
sodium	2%

Dandelion Greens with Tzatziki and Feta Cheese

Dandelion greens are considered to be weeds to some people, but they are a truly delicious spring green. They are very healthy—super-rich in vitamins A and K, calcium, and iron—and they taste fantastic in this Greek-style dish with feta cheese and tzatziki.

makes 4 main course or 6 side dish servings

3 tablespoons unsalted butter

6 tablespoons olive oil, divided

1 cup chopped onion

2 pounds dandelion greens, well-rinsed and trimmed

Kosher salt

$\frac{1}{2}$ cup chicken or vegetable broth

$1\frac{1}{2}$ cups Greek yogurt

1 cup seeded and grated cucumber

1 large garlic clove, minced

$\frac{1}{4}$ cup torn fresh mint leaves

2 tablespoons fresh lemon juice, divided

1 cup crumbled feta cheese

1. Heat the butter and 4 tablespoons of the olive oil in a large skillet over medium heat. Add the onion, reduce the heat, and sauté over low heat until they caramelize, about 30 minutes.

2. Add the dandelion greens with the water still clinging to the leaves to the onion. Add salt to taste. Cover the pan and simmer over very low heat for at least 30 minutes. Add a bit of broth if they seem too dry.

3. In a medium bowl, mix together the yogurt, cucumber, garlic, and mint leaves. Whisk the remaining 2 tablespoons olive oil and 1 tablespoon of the lemon juice together and add to yogurt mixture. Stir until it is well incorporated and creamy.

4. Sprinkle the remaining tablespoon of lemon juice over the greens and toss to combine. Lift the greens out of the pan and drain in a colander. Arrange the greens in a circle around a round serving platter, leaving a well in the center. Spoon a generous amount of the tzatziki in the center of dish and sprinkle the crumbled feta on top of the greens.

escarole

Escarole is a member of the chicory family. It is also known as broad-leaved endive, Bavarian endive, Batavian endive, *grumolo, scarola,* and *scarole.* It is thought to have originated either in the Mediterranean or in India.

It is a winter green and is at its freshest and best in the cold weather months. Look for heads of escarole with bright green leaves and avoid any with thick, tough outer leaves. It will keep, unwashed, in a plastic bag in the refrigerator for up to a week.

Escarole has a slightly bitter taste, similar to radicchio, and is a sprightly addition to the salad bowl and the soup pot. It is also an excellent green to sauté or braise. And since escarole leaves hold their shape well, they are great to stuff with ricotta cheese, raisins, and nuts and serve as a delicious side dish or entrée.

Escarole Soup

What could be better on a chilly day than a bowlful of hot soup made with fresh escarole and warm toasted bread and cheese?

makes 6 servings

3 tablespoons olive oil

3 flat anchovies

2 garlic cloves, minced

Pinch of red pepper flakes

1 large head (about 1¹/₂ pounds) escarole, washed and chopped

6 cups chicken stock

¹/₂ loaf Italian or French bread, cut into 1-inch-thick slices

¹/₂ cup freshly grated Parmesan cheese

1. Heat the olive oil in a large heavy soup pot over medium heat. Add the anchovies and mash with the back of a wooden spoon until they have dissolved into the olive oil. Add the garlic and red pepper flakes and sauté just until fragrant. Do not burn the garlic. Add the washed escarole with the water that is clinging to the leaves. Turn the leaves over several times with tongs until they are well covered with the oil and begin to wilt, about 2 minutes. Add the stock and bring to a very slow simmer. Reduce the heat to low and cook for about 30 minutes.

2. Meanwhile, put the bread slices on a baking sheet and brush both sides with olive oil. Put under the broiler and toast one side. Turn the bread slices over and sprinkle generously with the cheese. Put back under the broiler until the tops are well toasted.

3. Put the bread in flat soup bowls, ladle the soup over the bread, and serve at once.

Wilted Escarole and Bacon

Slightly bitter escarole gets a nice kick from garlic and red pepper flakes in this quickly sautéed dish.

makes 6 servings
1 large head (about 1$^{1}/_{2}$ pounds) escarole
2 slices thick-cut bacon
2 tablespoons olive oil
3 garlic cloves, thinly sliced
Pinch of red pepper flakes
2 teaspoons balsamic vinegar
1 tablespoon fresh lemon juice
Kosher salt and freshly ground black pepper

1. Remove any tough outer leaves and the core of the escarole. Separate the leaves and tear into 2-inch pieces. Wash well and dry thoroughly.

2. Cook the bacon until crisp in a large skillet over medium heat. Remove and drain on paper towels.

3. Pour off all but 1 tablespoon of the bacon fat. Add the olive oil and heat over medium heat. Add the garlic and red pepper flakes and sauté until the garlic is softened, 2 to 3 minutes. Add the escarole and cook, stirring occasionally, until it is wilted, about 5 minutes. Add the vinegar, lemon juice, and salt and pepper to taste and cook for 1 to 2 minutes. Taste and adjust the seasonings, if necessary. Crumble the bacon and sprinkle over the escarole. Serve at once.

Escarole is high in folic acid, fiber, and vitamin A. It is said to help the body heal infections.

One cup of cooked escarole has approximately:

calories	27.3
carbohydrates	1.8g
protein	1.5g
fat	1.8g

Of the recommended daily value, this portion provides:

vitamin A	43%
vitamin C	7%
vitamin B6	11%
folate	9%
niacin	12%
pantothenic acid	2%
calcium	3%
iron	4%
magnesium	1%
manganese	62%
potassium	8%
phosphorous	8%
copper	19%
selenium	1%
sodium	4%

Escarole Bundles with Tomato and Olive Sauce

Here is a fantastic dish of escarole leaves stuffed with ricotta cheese and raisins and topped with a savory tomato and olive sauce. This is wonderful to serve with roast chicken.

makes 6 servings

sauce:

2 tablespoons olive oil

1 can (16 ounces) small diced tomatoes

1 teaspoon sugar

1 teaspoon salt

$1/2$ cup chopped green olives, such as Manzanilla

1 large head (about $1^1/2$ pounds) escarole, washed

filling:

1 cup ricotta cheese

$1/3$ cup freshly grated Parmesan cheese, plus more for sprinkling

1 egg, lightly beaten

$1/2$ cup raisins

Kosher salt and freshly ground black pepper

1. To make the sauce, in a large sauté pan, heat the olive oil over medium heat. Add the tomatoes and their juices, sugar, salt, and olives. Cook at a low simmer until it thickens into a sauce, about 20 minutes. Set aside.

2. Meanwhile, bring a large pot of water to a boil. Carefully separate the escarole leaves. There should be 12 to 16 leaves. Drop them, about four at a time, into the pot and blanch for 1 minute. Put a clean, dry dish towel on a baking sheet. Remove the leaves individually with tongs and lay them on the towel.

3. To make the filling, in a medium bowl, mix together the cheeses, egg, raisins, and salt and pepper to taste.

4. Lay out a sheet of waxed paper and put 1 escarole leaf on it. At the stem end, place 1 tablespoon of the filling at about 1 inch from the end. Fold over the stem and begin to roll up the filling, folding the sides over to enclose the filling. Repeat with the remaining escarole leaves and filling.

5. Preheat the oven to 350°F. Spread about $1/4$ cup of the sauce on the bottom of a 9-inch pie plate or baking dish. Arrange the bundles snugly over the sauce. Spoon the remaining sauce over the top of the bundles and sprinkle with additional Parmesan cheese. Bake for 30 minutes. Serve at once.

Escarole Bundles with Creamy Sage Sauce

Here's a delicious variation of Escarole Bundles made with a warm and creamy sage sauce. We can't decide which one we love the most.

makes 6 servings

sauce:

2 cups heavy cream

2 tablespoons fresh sage leaves, thinly sliced

1/2 cup grated Gruyère cheese

1 large head (about 1 1/2 pounds) of escarole, washed

filling:

1 cup ricotta cheese

1 egg, lightly beaten

1/2 cup chopped walnuts

Kosher salt and freshly ground black pepper

topping:

4 tablespoons (1/2 stick) butter, melted

1/2 cup dry breadcrumbs

Kosher salt and freshly ground black pepper

1. To make the sauce, heat the cream and the sage leaves in a heavy-bottomed saucepan until barely simmering. Add the Gruyère cheese and stir until melted. Set aside.

2. Bring a large pot of water to a boil. Carefully separate the escarole leaves. There should be 12 to 16 leaves. Drop them, about four at a time, into the pot and blanch for 1 minute. Put a clean, dry dish towel on a baking sheet. Remove the leaves individually with tongs and lay them on the towel.

3. Preheat the oven to 350°F.

4. To make the filling, in a medium bowl, mix together the ricotta cheese, egg, walnuts, and salt and pepper to taste. Lay out a sheet of waxed paper and put 1 escarole leaf on it. At the stem end, place 1 tablespoon of the filling at about 1 inch from the end. Fold over the stem and begin to roll up the filling, folding the sides over to enclose the filling. Repeat with the remaining escarole leaves and filling. Arrange the bundles in a pie plate or baking dish. Pour the sauce over the escarole bundles.

5. To make the topping, stir the melted butter, breadcrumbs, and salt and pepper to taste until combined. Sprinkle the crumbs over the bundles and bake for 30 minutes. Serve at once.

fennel

Beautiful pale-green fennel, also known as anise or finocchio, is often mistaken for celery, but its licorice flavor and crunchy texture are entirely its own. It originated in southern Europe and the Mediterranean region.

Fennel is available year-round and is at its peak in the fall and winter months. When buying fennel, look for bulbs with their stalks intact, complete within the feathery fronds. Press the flesh of the bulb to test for freshness; it should feel firm and resist gentle pressure. Pass on any bulbs that feel soft. Although it is best to use it right away, fennel will keep in the refrigerator, wrapped in plastic, for up to three days.

Fennel is wonderful to eat raw with olive oil and salt, or with a crumbly cheese. It takes beautifully to slow roasting and braising, and it is a perfect accompaniment to all types of fish and meat.

Braised Fennel Soup

We like to braise fennel in the oven with onions, potatoes, and carrots until they become very tender before puréeing it into this rich and aromatic soup.

makes 6 servings

2 medium fennel bulbs (about 1¼ pounds)

3 tablespoons olive oil

3 garlic cloves, thinly sliced

1 medium onion, coarsely chopped

1 medium Yukon Gold or other firm white potato, peeled and cubed

2 medium carrots, peeled and diced

8 sprigs fresh flat-leaf parsley

Pinch of dried thyme

2 tablespoons unsalted butter, cut into small pieces

6 cups chicken or vegetable broth

Kosher salt and freshly ground black pepper

1 teaspoon Pernod liqueur or Jägermeister

1 cup half and half

1. Preheat the oven to 350°F. Trim the fronds from the fennel, chop them, and set aside. Core and halve or quarter the bulbs.

2. Coat the bottom of a large roasting pan with the olive oil. Put the fennel bulbs, garlic, onion, potato, and carrots in the pan. Add the parsley sprigs and sprinkle with thyme. Dot with the butter and pour the stock over the vegetables. Season with salt and pepper to taste. Cover the pan tightly with aluminum foil and roast for about 1 hour. Remove the foil and bake another 15 minutes, or until the vegetables are very tender. If the vegetables are dry, add a little more stock or water during the last 15 minutes of roasting. Let the vegetables cool in the pan.

3. Transfer the vegetables to a food processor fitted with a metal blade and purée until smooth. You will have to do this in batches. Put the purée in a large saucepan or stockpot and cook over medium-low heat. Stir in the Pernod and half-and-half and let the soup get as hot as possible without boiling. Adjust the seasoning and reheat gently, if necessary.

4. To serve, ladle the soup into bowls, sprinkle with the chopped fennel fronds, and serve at once.

Fennel and Orange Salad

This cool, crunchy salad, made with thin slices of fennel and oranges, is very refreshing. It's just the thing to serve at a summer picnic or barbecue.

makes 4 to 6 servings
1 large or 2 medium fennel bulbs, trimmed and julienned
½ red onion, thinly sliced
1 teaspoon balsamic vinegar
2 tablespoons soy sauce
1 tablespoon orange juice
1 tablespoon minced fresh ginger
⅓ cup olive oil
Kosher salt and freshly ground black pepper
1 medium orange, peeled
1 tablespoon fresh lemon juice

1. Put the fennel and onion in a large bowl.

2. Whisk together the vinegar, soy sauce, orange juice, ginger, and olive oil in a small bowl. Pour over the fennel and onion and toss well. Season to taste with salt and pepper. Chill the salad for 1 hour.

3. Slice the peeled orange into thin round "wheels" and slice each wheel into half. Add the orange slices and lemon juice and toss. Taste and adjust the seasonings, if necessary, and serve.

Roasted Fennel, Pears, and Mixed Greens Salad

This lovely autumnal salad of slow-roasted fennel and pears tastes as good as it looks.

makes 6 servings

salad:

2 tablespoons corn oil

1 fennel bulb, trimmed and thinly sliced

2 ripe Red Bartlett or Bosc pears, quartered, cored, and thinly sliced

2 large heads endive

4 cups mixed salad greens

vinaigrette:

2 tablespoons red wine vinegar

$\frac{1}{3}$ cup extra-virgin olive oil

1 teaspoon herbes de Provence

Kosher salt and freshly ground black pepper

$\frac{1}{2}$ cup shaved fresh Parmesan cheese, for garnish

1. Preheat the oven to 350°F.

2. To make the salad, brush a baking sheet with 1 tablespoon of the corn oil. Add the fennel, toss to coat, and spread in an even layer. Brush a second baking sheet with the remaining 1 tablespoon corn oil. Add the pears, toss to coat, and spread in an even layer. Bake the fennel and the pears until tender, about 30 minutes.

3. Trim off the base of the endives, separate the leaves, and tear in half. Combine the endive and mixed salad greens in a large salad bowl and toss together.

4. To make the vinaigrette, in a small bowl whisk together the vinegar and olive oil. Add the herbes de Provence and salt and pepper to taste and whisk well to combine. Pour half of the vinaigrette over the endive and greens and toss gently to coat.

5. Serve from the bowl or arrange on individual plates. Top with the roasted fennel and pears and drizzle with the remaining vinaigrette. Garnish with Parmesan shavings and additional ground pepper, if desired, and serve at once.

Slow-Roasted Fennel with Feta Cheese

The subtle flavor of fennel is enhanced when it is slow-roasted with olive oil and topped with feta cheese, fresh breadcrumbs, and black olives.

makes 6 servings

3 tablespoons olive oil, divided

2 fennel bulbs, trimmed

$1/2$ cup crumbled feta cheese

$1/2$ cup fresh breadcrumbs

$1/4$ cup kalamata olives, pitted and halved

Freshly ground black pepper

1. Preheat the oven to 350°F. Brush the bottom of a large baking dish with 1 tablespoon of the olive oil.

2. Cut the fennel into $1/4$-inch-thick slices. Cut the slices in half lengthwise and layer in the baking dish. Brush the tops of the fennel slices with the remaining 2 tablespoons olive oil. Bake for 30 minutes. Remove from the oven, turn the fennel slices, and return to the oven. Bake for 30 more minutes.

3. Remove the fennel from the oven, sprinkle the top evenly with the cheese and breadcrumbs, and dot with the olives. Season generously with black pepper to taste and bake until the cheese melts, about 10 minutes.

4. Preheat the broiler and broil until the top is browned and bubbly, about 3 minutes. Serve hot or at room temperature.

Fennel is a stimulant and one of the three main herbs used to make absinthe. It is also a carminative, which is an herb that prevents gas in the gastrointestinal tract.

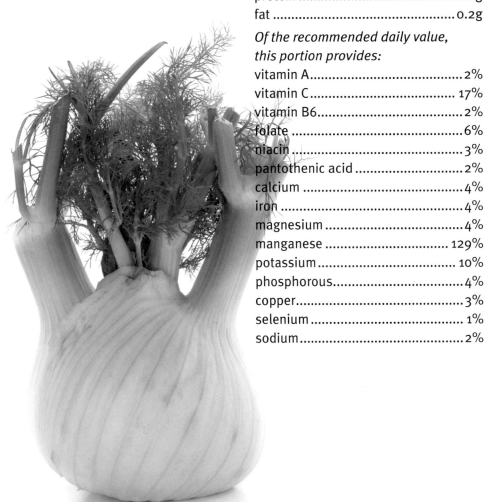

One cup of raw fennel
has approximately:

calories 27
carbohydrates.............................. 6.3g
protein 1.1g
fat 0.2g

Of the recommended daily value,
this portion provides:

vitamin A.. 2%
vitamin C 17%
vitamin B6...................................... 2%
folate 6%
niacin 3%
pantothenic acid 2%
calcium 4%
iron 4%
magnesium 4%
manganese 129%
potassium 10%
phosphorous.................................. 4%
copper.. 3%
selenium 1%
sodium... 2%

Roast Pork with Fennel and Onions

This delectable dish of pork roasted with fennel, onions, and herbs is wonderful to serve for a small dinner party.

makes 4 to 6 servings

1 boneless pork loin (about 2½ pounds)

Kosher salt and freshly ground black pepper

2 tablespoons olive oil

2 onions, coarsely chopped

6 garlic cloves, thinly sliced

1 fennel bulb, trimmed and coarsely chopped

2 sprigs fresh rosemary

2 sprigs fresh thyme

¼ cup white wine

¼ cup chicken broth

1. Preheat the oven to 350°F.

2. Season the pork on all sides with salt and pepper. Heat the olive oil over medium heat in a large ovenproof soup pot or Dutch oven. Brown the pork on all sides, about 6 minutes total, and then transfer to a plate. Add the onions and garlic to the pot and sauté until softened, stirring occasionally, for about 7 minutes. Add the fennel, rosemary, and thyme and sauté for 1 minute.

3. Add the wine and broth to the pot and bring to a boil. Turn off the heat and return the meat to the pot. Cover and bake in the oven for 1 hour.

4. Remove the pork and let sit for 5 to 10 minutes before carving. Cut the pork into ½-inch-thick slices.

5. Remove the rosemary and thyme sprigs from the fennel and onion mixture. Taste and adjust the seasonings, if necessary. Serve with the sliced pork.

Grilled Garlic Scapes

The first sign of springtime for me is the moment my garlic shoots start poking up out of the dismal brown earth. Once they reach up to about a foot and a half the beautiful scapes start twisting up out of each plant. They're curvy and graceful, like the neck of a swan. You need to cut them as soon as they make that first loop. Do it fast because it only happens once and it is such a treat. Once the scapes are cooked they become soft and creamy with a faint sweet taste of garlic.

They're easy to make. Pour 1 tablespoon of olive oil into the palm of your hand, and then rub the scapes with the oil and place them on a hot grill. Sprinkle with kosher salt, and cook until they become lightly brown, about 2 minutes. Turn them over and grill 2 more minutes. Remove to a bowl, cover with a plate or foil, and let them steam for 5 minutes or so.

There are so many ways to serve them. Here are just a few:

- Cut them into 2-inch pieces and serve as a side dish sprinkled with chopped chives.

- Serve them as a pretty pile tangled on top of grilled steak, or as a bed underneath grilled or roasted chicken.

- Chop and toss together with pasta, melted butter, and a squeeze of lemon.

- Slice them on a cutting board and eat them with your fingers with a glass of Prosecco at your first outdoor party of the season. Cheers!

herbs

Fresh herbs are essential to good cooking. A generous handful of chopped fresh herbs will enhance any dish and add great flavor, color, and texture to it. All types of herbs are very easy to grow in gardens, window boxes, and pots in the kitchen—so there is no good reason not to always have them on hand.

Ideally, leafy herbs should be stored in the refrigerator in a glass, stem side down, in about an inch of water. The top of the herbs should be loosely covered with a perforated plastic bag. They should never be stored in an airtight bag. Woody herbs, like sage, rosemary, and thyme, can be stored in the refrigerator loosely wrapped in plastic or in a perforated plastic bag.

In addition to adding fresh herbs to a variety of dishes at the end of cooking or using them as a garnish, we also use them to make fantastic pesto, sauces, salsas, marinades, and butters.

Classic Basil Pesto

The classic aromatic blend of fresh basil leaves, garlic, nuts, and olive oil is a welcome summer staple in our kitchens.

makes about 1 cup

1 cup fresh basil leaves

2 garlic cloves, peeled

$1/2$ cup pine nuts or walnuts

$1/2$ cup olive oil

$1/4$ cup freshly grated Parmesan cheese

Kosher salt
   and freshly ground black pepper

Put the basil, garlic, and nuts in a food processor or blender and process until finely chopped. Leave the motor running and add the oil in a slow, steady stream. Transfer to a bowl and stir in the cheese and salt and pepper to taste. Taste and adjust the seasonings, if necessary. The sauce will keep, covered, in the refrigerator for up to two days. Bring to room temperature and stir well before serving.

Basil and Mint Pesto

Fresh mint adds a nice touch to pesto sauce. This is lovely with fresh pasta.

makes about 1 1/2 cups

$1/2$ cup, plus 1 tablespoon olive oil, divided

2 garlic cloves, peeled

$1/4$ cup chopped pine nuts

1 cup fresh basil

$1/2$ cup chopped fresh flat-leaf parsley

$1/2$ cup fresh mint

1 tablespoon fresh lemon juice

Kosher salt
   and freshly ground black pepper

Heat 1 tablespoon of the olive oil in a small sauté pan over medium heat and cook the garlic until golden, about 5 minutes. Transfer to a food processor. Add the pine nuts, basil, parsley, and mint to the food processor and process. Leave the motor running and add the remaining $1/2$ cup olive oil in a slow, steady stream. Process until very smooth. Add the lemon juice and salt and pepper to taste. The sauce will keep, covered, in the refrigerator for up to two days. Bring to room temperature and stir well before serving.

Olive Pesto

This pesto variation is great to spread on grilled bread and it's also a good accompaniment to grilled fish.

makes about 1 cup

$1/2$ cup fresh basil leaves

$1/4$ cup fresh flat-leaf parsley

2 garlic cloves, peeled

2 shallots, chopped

2 tablespoons walnuts

$1/2$ cup chopped black olives

$1/4$ cup olive oil

2 tablespoons freshly grated
  Parmesan cheese

Freshly ground black pepper

Put the basil, parsley, garlic, shallots, walnuts, and olives in a food processor or blender and process until finely chopped. Leave the motor running and add the oil in a slow, steady stream. Transfer to a bowl and stir in the cheese and pepper to taste. Taste and adjust the seasonings, if necessary. The sauce will keep, covered, in the refrigerator for up to two days. Bring to room temperature and stir well before serving.

Basil Salsa Verde

This piquant green sauce is a terrific accompaniment to slow-roasted meats and stews.

makes about 1 1/4 cups

$1/2$ cup basil leaves

1 cup chopped fresh flat-leaf parsley

1 garlic clove, peeled

2 teaspoons red wine vinegar

1 tablespoon drained capers

1 teaspoon Dijon mustard

4 canned anchovy fillets,
  drained and chopped

$1/2$ cup olive oil

Freshly ground black pepper

Put the basil, parsley, garlic, vinegar, capers, mustard, and anchovies in a food processor and process until blended. Leave the motor running and add the oil in a slow, steady stream. Process until smooth, adding more oil if the sauce seems too thick. Season to taste with pepper. Let the sauce stand at room temperature for 1 to 2 hours before serving.

Dill and Parsley Pesto

This pesto is excellent to add to potato salad or grilled or steamed vegetables.

makes about 1 cup

1$^1/_2$ cups chopped fresh dill

$^1/_2$ cup chopped fresh flat-leaf parsley

2 garlic cloves, peeled

2 tablespoons pine nuts or walnuts

$^1/_4$ cup olive oil

2 tablespoons freshly grated
  Parmesan cheese

Kosher salt
  and freshly ground black pepper

Put the dill, parsley, garlic, and nuts in a food processor or blender and process until finely chopped. Leave the motor running and add the oil in a slow, steady stream. Transfer to a bowl and stir in the cheese and salt and pepper to taste. The sauce will keep, covered, in the refrigerator for up to two days. Bring to room temperature and stir well before serving.

Dill Sauce

This is the best sauce for smoked salmon on pumpernickel toasts. Trust us.

makes 1/2 cup

$^1/_2$ cup mayonnaise

2 teaspoons Dijon mustard

2 tablespoons chopped fresh dill

2 teaspoons whole milk

Pinch of sugar

Combine the mayonnaise, mustard, and dill in a small bowl and mix together. Add the milk and sugar and mix again. Taste and adjust the seasonings, if necessary. The sauce will keep, covered, in the refrigerator for up to three days.

Mustard-Dill Sauce

This sauce uses a generous amount of dill and it is excellent with any grilled, poached, or broiled fish.

makes about 1 1/4 cups

1/4 cup coarse whole grain mustard

1 1/2 tablespoons sugar

2 tablespoon white wine vinegar

1 cup safflower oil

1 small bunch fresh dill,
  stemmed and chopped

Kosher salt
  and freshly ground black pepper

Whisk together the mustard, sugar, and vinegar in a small bowl. Add the oil in a thin stream, whisking constantly, until the sauce emulsifies. Whisk in the dill and salt and pepper to taste. The sauce will keep, covered, in the refrigerator for up to two days. Bring to room temperature and stir well before serving.

Dill, Scallion, and Walnut Sauce

We love this elegant sauce. It brings a fresh and bright flavor to salmon or tuna and it's also excellent tossed with fresh green beans.

makes about 1 cup

1/2 cup chopped fresh dill

1/4 cup chopped fresh flat-leaf parsley

1/2 cup chopped scallions

1/3 cup walnuts

1 tablespoon cider vinegar

1/2 cup walnut oil

Kosher salt
  and freshly ground black pepper

Put the dill, parsley, scallions, walnuts, vinegar, oil, and salt and pepper to taste in a blender and blend until smooth. Taste and adjust the seasonings, if necessary. The sauce will keep, covered, in the refrigerator for up to three days. Bring to room temperature and stir well before serving.

Mint and Vinegar Dipping Sauce

Drizzle this fantastic sauce over grilled chicken, lamb, or fish.

makes about 3/4 cup

1/2 cup chopped fresh mint

2 garlic cloves, minced

1 small red chile, seeded and minced, or 1/2 teaspoon red pepper flakes

2 tablespoons cider vinegar

1 tablespoon low-sodium soy sauce

1 tablespoon sherry

1 teaspoon sugar

1 tablespoon olive oil

1/2 teaspoon hot sauce

1 to 2 tablespoons water

Put the mint, garlic, chile, vinegar, soy sauce, sherry, sugar, olive oil, hot sauce, and 1 tablespoon of water in a bowl and whisk until blended. Taste and adjust the seasonings, adding more water, if necessary. The sauce will keep in the refrigerator for about two days. When ready to use, bring to room temperature and whisk before serving.

Mint and Parsley Salsa Verde

This is a nice accompaniment to lamb and pork as well as spicy dishes.

makes about 1 1/2 cups

3/4 cup chopped fresh mint

3/4 cup chopped fresh flat-leaf parsley

2 shallots, chopped

2 garlic cloves, peeled

2 tablespoons sherry vinegar

1 to 2 tablespoons water

1/2 cup olive oil

Put the mint, parsley, shallots, garlic, vinegar, and 1 tablespoon of water in a food processor and process until finely chopped. Leave the motor running and add the oil in a slow, steady stream. Taste and adjust the seasonings, adding more water, if necessary. The sauce will keep in the refrigerator for two days.

Parsley and Basil Sauce

This easy-to-make sauce brings fresh and bright flavor to all types of dishes.

makes about 3/4 cup

3 tablespoons olive oil

3 garlic cloves, thinly sliced

2 shallots, thinly sliced

1 cup coarsely chopped fresh basil

$1/2$ cup chopped fresh flat-leaf parsley

1 teaspoon fresh lemon juice

$1/2$ cup extra-virgin olive oil

Kosher salt
  and freshly ground black pepper

Heat the oil in a small sauté pan. Add the garlic and shallots and cook until softened, about 5 minutes. Transfer to a food processor. Add the basil, parsley, and lemon juice and process until well combined. Leave the motor running and add the oil in a slow, steady stream. Add the salt and pepper to taste and process again. Taste and adjust the seasonings, if necessary. The sauce will keep, covered, in the refrigerator for up to three days. Bring to room temperature and stir well before serving.

Chimichurri Sauce

Chimichurri is a classic accompaniment to serve with grilled skirt steak—it's really great with all types of grilled meat.

makes about 1 cup

1 cup coarsely chopped fresh
  flat-leaf parsley

5 garlic cloves, peeled

$1/2$ cup olive oil

2 tablespoons red wine vinegar

Pinch of red pepper flakes

Kosher salt
  and freshly ground black pepper

Put the parsley and garlic in a food processor and process until blended. Leave the motor running and add the oil in a slow, steady stream. Add the vinegar, red pepper flakes, and salt and pepper to taste and process again. The sauce will keep, covered, in the refrigerator for up to two days. Bring it to room temperature and stir well before serving.

Fresh Herb and Lemon Marinade

This marinade is packed with fresh flavor. We like to marinate steaks in it for a few hours before grilling.

makes about 1 cup

$1/2$ cup chopped fresh flat-leaf parsley
$1/4$ cup chopped fresh thyme
$1/4$ cup chopped fresh rosemary
1 tablespoon chopped fresh sage
6 garlic cloves, peeled
Juice of 1 lemon
$3/4$ cup olive oil

Put the parsley, thyme, rosemary, sage, garlic, and lemon juice in a food processor and process until blended. Leave the motor running and add the oil in a slow, steady stream and process until very smooth. The marinade will keep, covered, in the refrigerator for up to two days. Bring it to room temperature and stir well before using.

Herb Butters

Soft butter mixed with fresh herbs, spices, or cheese makes a wonderful spread for grilled vegetables, corn on the cob, and bread. Here are a few ideas for tasty herb butters.

Mint-Feta Butter

makes about 3/4 cup

4 tablespoons ($1/2$ stick) unsalted butter, at room temperature
$1/2$ cup crumbled feta cheese
$1/4$ cup finely chopped fresh mint
Freshly ground black pepper

Put the butter in a small bowl. Add the cheese and mint and mash with a fork until mixed. Season to taste with pepper.

Basil-Parmesan Butter

makes about 3/4 cup

4 tablespoons ($^1/_2$ stick) unsalted butter,
  at room temperature

$^1/_2$ cup freshly grated Parmesan cheese

$^1/_4$ cup finely chopped fresh basil

Kosher salt
  and freshly ground black pepper

Put the butter in a small bowl. Add the
cheese and basil and mash with a fork until
mixed. Season to taste with salt and pepper.

Herbed Shallot Butter

makes about 3/4 cup

4 tablespoons ($^1/_2$ stick) unsalted butter,
  at room temperature

2 teaspoons finely chopped shallots

2 teapoons chopped fresh flat-leaf parsley

2 teapoons snipped fresh chives

Freshly ground black pepper

Put the butter in a small bowl. Add the shallots, parsley, and chives and mash with a fork
until mixed. Season to taste with pepper.

Cilantro-Cumin Butter

makes about 3/4 cup

4 tablespoons ($^1/_2$ stick) unsalted butter,
  at room temperature

1 garlic clove, finely minced

$^1/_4$ cup finely chopped fresh cilantro

1 tablespoon ground cumin

Kosher salt
  and freshly ground black pepper

Put the butter in a small bowl. Add the
garlic, cilantro, and cumin and mash with a
fork until mixed. Season to taste with salt
and pepper.

kale

Kale is a member of the *brassica oleracea* family whose members also include broccoli, cauliflower, and collards. It is a descendent of the wild cabbage that is thought to have originated in Asia Minor. English settlers brought it to this country in the seventeenth century.

It is available throughout the year and is at its peak from mid-winter through April or May. Look for kale with moist-looking, dark green leaves and pass on any with brown or yellow leaves. To store kale, wrap it in a damp paper towel and put it in a plastic bag in the refrigerator for up to two days. The longer it is stored the more bitter it becomes.

Kale's robust flavor and peppery kick taste great with bold ingredients, such as red pepper flakes, chilies, vinegar, or bacon. This dark leafy green is one to savor. Not only is it very healthy, it also tastes fantastic.

Crispy Kale Chips

When kale is slow roasted in the oven it becomes crispy and has a very nutty flavor. These kale chips are a terrific snack to serve with cocktails or wine.

makes 6 servings

1 bunch kale, stemmed, rinsed, and thoroughly dried

2 to 3 tablespoons olive oil

Kosher salt and freshly ground black pepper

1. Preheat the oven to 250°F.

2. Tear the kale into 2^1/$_2$ to 3-inch pieces and put them in a large bowl. Toss with the olive oil and salt and pepper to taste, making sure that the leaves are well coated with the oil. Arrange the leaves in a single layer on two baking sheets.

3. Bake until crisp, tossing once or twice, for 30 to 35 minutes. Serve at once.

Kale has more nutritional value for fewer calories than almost any other food. Kale is high in beta-carotene, lutein, and zeaxanthin and has antioxidants.

One head of cooked kale has approximately:

calories	27
carbohydrates	6.3g
protein	1.1g
fat	0.2g

Of the recommended daily value, this portion provides:

vitamin A	2%
vitamin C	17%
vitamin B6	2%
folate	6%
niacin	3%
pantothenic acid	2%
calcium	4%
iron	4%
magnesium	4%
manganese	8%
potassium	10%
phosphorous	4%
copper	3%
selenium	1%
sodium	2%

Kale, Sweet Potato, and Orzo Soup

Deep green kale and orange sweet potatoes are a healthy and wonderful combination. This soup is a good one to play with since you can add other greens such as spinach, collard greens, or watercress and substitute another small pasta for the orzo. A delicious bowlful of this soup will really take the chill out of a wintry day.

makes 8 to 10 servings

6 cups chicken or vegetable broth

2 cups water

$1/2$ pound kale, tough ends trimmed, chopped into $1/2$-inch pieces

2 sweet potatoes, peeled and cut into $1/2$-inch dice

$1/2$ cup orzo or small pasta

Freshly ground black pepper

Parmesan cheese, for serving (optional)

1. Put the broth, water, kale, and sweet potatoes in a large soup pot and bring to a boil. Reduce the heat, cover, and simmer gently until the potatoes are fork-tender, 15 to 20 minutes.

2. Meanwhile, bring a pan of water to a boil. Add the orzo and cook until just tender. Drain and set aside.

3. Add the orzo and pepper to taste to the soup pot. Cover and cook over low heat for 10 minutes longer. Serve immediately with Parmesan cheese, if desired.

Kale and Cannellini

Kale is a very hardy plant that can tolerate almost any kind of soil as long as it has good drainage. It loves cool weather and can be harvested through most of the fall here in the Northeast. We love the combination of strong-flavored, robust greens with creamy white beans in this dish.

makes 6 servings

¹/₄ cup olive oil

1 cup thinly sliced shallots

2 large bunches kale, about 1 pound each

2 teaspoons kosher salt

2 cups vegetable broth

2 cans (15.5 ounces) cannellini beans, rinsed and drained

1 can (28 ounces) diced tomatoes

1 can (3 ounces) green chilies

1. In a large heavy-bottomed pot, heat the olive oil and add the shallots. Cook over very low heat for 15 minutes, until they begin to caramelize. Do not let them burn.

2. Meanwhile, wash the kale in several changes of cold water. Tear off the leafy parts from the thick stalks. Add the leaves to the pot and turn up the heat to medium. With tongs, turn the leaves over several times to coat with the olive oil and to mix in the shallots. Sprinkle with the salt and add the broth. Cover the pot and simmer gently for 20 minutes, stirring occasionally.

3. Add the beans, tomatoes and their juices, and chilies. Simmer, partially covered, for 15 minutes, stirring occasionally. Ladle into individual soup bowls and serve with warm buttered country bread.

leeks

Leeks are members of the onion family *(allium porrum)*. They are thought to have originated in the Mediterranean region and Asia and have been cultivated for more than three thousand years.

They are available year-round and are at their best from September through the end of April. Although very big leeks are fine for soup, the best leeks to select are never more than 1 $^1/_2$ to 2 inches in diameter. Slender, younger leeks have a more delicate flavor and cook quickly. To store them, they should be lightly wrapped in plastic, unwashed, and put in the refrigerator. Depending on their freshness when purchased, they will keep for up to a week or two.

Although cleaning leeks can be fairly labor intensive, the results are well worth it. They have a sweet and delicate flavor that is subtler than onions. They're delicious in soups, drizzled with vinaigrette, or braised in broth or white wine.

Herbed Leek and Watercress Soup

This lovely soup is made with fresh leeks, watercress, and basil, and it's just the thing to serve as a starter for a spring dinner.

makes 4 servings

2 large russet potatoes, peeled and diced

3½ cups chicken broth

1 tablespoon unsalted butter

1 tablespoon olive oil

1 onion, diced

2 leeks, rinsed, dried, and diced

3 scallions, trimmed and minced

1 bunch watercress, rinsed and stemmed

½ cup basil leaves, thinly sliced, divided

½ teaspoon ground nutmeg

Freshly ground black pepper to taste

1 cup whole milk

1. Place the potatoes and broth in a large soup pot and bring to a boil. Reduce the heat and simmer, partially covered, until the potatoes are just tender, 10 to 15 minutes.

2. Meanwhile, heat the butter and oil over medium-low heat in a large sauté pan. Add the onion and leeks and cook until tender, about 10 minutes. Add the scallions and watercress and cook for 5 more minutes.

3. Add the vegetable mixture, ¼ cup of the basil, the nutmeg, and pepper to the soup. Cook, stirring occasionally, for 5 minutes then set aside to cool.

4. Purée the soup in batches in a blender or food processor until very smooth. Return the soup to the pot. Just before serving, stir in the milk and heat through over low heat. Taste and adjust the seasonings. Serve garnished with the remaining ¼ cup basil.

Leeks Vinaigrette

This is an elegant leek dish that can be served warm, cold, or at room temperature. We use canola oil in the vinaigrette that gives it a very light flavor.

makes 4 to 6 servings
4 large leeks (about 2 pounds)
Kosher salt and freshly ground black pepper
1 tablespoon Dijon mustard
1 tablespoon red wine vinegar
⅓ cup canola oil
Dash of hot sauce
2 tablespoons chopped fresh flat-leaf parsley

1. Trim the root ends and the green tops off the leeks and split lengthwise. Rinse the leeks well under cold running water to remove all the dirt.

2. Put the leeks in a large pan. Add enough cold water to cover the leeks and salt and pepper. Bring to a boil and simmer until tender, about 10 minutes. Drain the leeks thoroughly. When cool enough to handle, press them between your hands to extract excess liquid.

3. Split the leeks in half lengthwise and then cut crosswise into 1½-inch pieces. Arrange them in a serving dish.

4. In a small bowl, whisk the mustard and vinegar together. Slowly add the canola oil and whisk constantly until emulsified. Add the hot sauce and salt and pepper to taste.

5. Spoon the sauce over the leeks and sprinkle with parsley.

Braised Leeks and Chickpeas

This simple preparation of leeks sautéed with chickpeas is an ideal complement to roast chicken or an omelet.

makes 4 to 6 servings

2 pounds leeks

2 tablespoons olive oil

2 shallots, thinly sliced

¼ cup chicken broth

1 can (15 ounces) chickpeas, drained

Kosher salt and freshly ground black pepper

1. Trim the dark green tops and the root ends from the leeks. Cut the leeks in half lengthwise, rinse thoroughly and pat dry, and then cut into 2-inch pieces.

2. Heat the oil in a large skillet over medium heat. Add the shallots and sauté until softened, about 3 minutes. Add the leeks and sauté, stirring often, until softened, 8 to 10 minutes.

3. Add half of the broth and cook, stirring occasionally, until it is absorbed. Add the remaining broth and cook until the rest of the broth is absorbed, about 5 minutes.

4. Add the chickpeas and stir to mix well. Season to taste with salt and pepper and cook, stirring, for 10 minutes. Serve warm. If not serving right away, cover the pan and gently reheat.

Oven-Braised Leeks and Garlic

Leeks are such a versatile vegetable. They are one of the few vegetables that can be harvested from the late-fall garden, even after a frost, and as such they taste wonderfully fresh throughout autumn and winter. A dish of these warm, oven-braised leeks is an excellent side to serve all winter long.

makes 6 servings
2 pounds leeks
2 tablespoons olive oil
6 garlic cloves, halved
3 or 4 tablespoons chicken broth
Kosher salt and freshly ground black pepper

1. Preheat the oven to 350°F.

2. Trim the dark green tops and the root ends from the leeks. Cut the leeks in half lengthwise, rinse thoroughly and pat dry, and then cut the halves crosswise into thirds.

3. Coat the bottom of a large baking dish with the olive oil and arrange the leeks and garlic halves in the dish. Drizzle 3 tablespoons of chicken broth over them and season to taste with salt and pepper.

4. Bake for about 45 minutes, until the leeks are tender but still offering some resistance. Add a little more broth if the leeks seem dry and bake for 15 minutes longer, until tender. Serve immediately.

Leeks raise the level of "good" cholesterol (HDL) and lower the level of "bad" cholesterol. Leeks help stabilize blood sugar and prevent colon, prostate, and ovarian cancers.

One leek (124g) has approximately:
calories 38
carbohydrates............................... 9.4g
protein 1g
fat 0.2g

Of the recommended daily value, this portion provides:
vitamin A......................................20%
vitamin C......................................9%
vitamin E......................................3%
vitamin K......................................39%
vitamin B6....................................7%

folate 7%
niacin 1%
pantothenic acid 1%
calcium 4%
iron 8%
magnesium 4%
manganese 15%
potassium 3%
phosphorous................................... 2%
copper... 4%
selenium 1%
sodium.. 1%

Prime Rib Roasted on a Bed of Leeks: Trim off the tough tops of the leeks, leaving some green. Slice them thinly lengthwise into long strips and wash them thoroughly to remove any sand. Toss in a large bowl with olive oil, kosher salt, and any water still clinging to them, and arrange in the bottom of a roasting pan. Drizzle a bit more oil on the leeks and put the rib roast directly over them. Cook the roast as you normally do, and once the roast is removed, sliced, and plated, pile a generous amount of the carmelized leeks on top of each slice and spoon a bit of the drippings from the pan over each pile. Man is this good!

Grilled Sirloin Steak
with Leek and Red Wine Sauce

Tender and flavorful grilled sirloin steak tastes great with rich and creamy leek and red wine sauce. Try this with roasted red potatoes.

makes 6 servings

2 pounds leeks

1 tablespoon unsalted butter

1 tablespoon olive oil

2 cups red wine

$1/4$ cup beef broth

Kosher salt and freshly ground black pepper

4 to 5 pounds boneless sirloin steak

1. Trim the dark green tops and the root ends from the leeks. Cut the leeks in half lengthwise, rinse thoroughly and pat dry, and then cut into $1/2$-inch pieces.

2. Heat the butter and oil in a large sauté pan over medium heat. Add the leeks and sauté, stirring often, until softened, 8 to 10 minutes. Add the wine and broth, reduce the heat, and simmer, stirring occasionally, for 20 minutes. Raise the heat, add salt and pepper to taste, and cook until the sauce is slightly thickened, about 5 minutes.

3. Prepare a medium-hot gas or charcoal grill. Generously season the steaks with salt and pepper and grill for 4 to 6 minutes per side for medium-rare, or until desired doneness. Let the steak rest for 10 minutes before slicing. Slice the steak, against the grain, into $1/4$-inch-thick slices and arrange on a platter. Reheat the leek sauce, if necessary, and spoon over the steak. Serve at once.

mixed greens

Mixed greens, such as kale, spinach, collards, dandelion, mustard greens, and Swiss chard, are available in their leafy splendor year-round, and they work very well when cooked together in almost any combination. A good way to cook them is to use a mixture of mild, semi-mild, and stronger-flavored greens together and experiment with different mixes.

All of these greens have a high water content and wilt easily, so search out bunches that have the freshest and greenest leaves and pass on any with yellow or discolored leaves. They can be stored in a plastic bag, unwashed, in the refrigerator for about five days.

Fresh greens shrink considerably when cooked and so the amount you begin with may seem disproportionately large. It isn't. Try these healthy and delicious greens in any combination and any number of ways—in a quick sauté or a slow braise, as a topping for homemade pizza, or served with fresh fish.

Sautéed Kale, Spinach, and Collard Greens

Fresh kale, spinach, and collards are simple to prepare, requiring only a large pan and a few minutes over good heat to wilt, release their liquid, and turn a gorgeous dark green. If you have a pan large enough, cook all of the greens at once; if not, cook them in two or three batches.

makes 6 to 8 servings
2 tablespoons olive oil
2 bunches (about 1 pound) fresh spinach, rinsed and stemmed
2 bunches (about 1 pound) collard greens, rinsed and stemmed
1 bunch (about 1 pound) green or purple kale, rinsed and stemmed
Kosher salt and freshly ground black pepper

1. In a large skillet, heat the oil over medium-high heat. Add as much spinach, collards, and kale as will fit in the pan and cook, stirring frequently, for about 5 minutes until the greens begin to wilt. Season to taste with salt and pepper and then lift the greens from the pan with tongs and set aside on a large plate or in a large bowl. Continue cooking the remaining greens, adding more oil to the pan, if necessary. When all the greens are wilted, return them to the pan and stir to mix.

2. Cover the pan and steam the greens over medium-high heat for about 1 minute. Uncover and cook for a few minutes longer until any liquid evaporates. Adjust the seasonings with salt and pepper, toss, and serve immediately.

Note: Greens that have not been picked fresh from a garden may taste bitter. If you suspect the greens you are cooking are not fresh, plunge them in boiling water for about 1 minute before draining and sautéing. This will remove any bitterness.

Mixed Greens Gumbo

Although most gumbos are made with shrimp or sausage, here's a gumbo recipe that is made with fresh mixed greens, such as mustard or collard greens, kale, spinach, or Swiss chard, and filé powder (see note). This very tasty vegetarian dish should be served over hot rice and with hot sauce on the side.

makes 8 servings
1/4 cup vegetable oil
1/4 cup flour
3 yellow onions, chopped
3 celery ribs, chopped
1 green bell pepper, cored, seeded, and chopped
4 garlic cloves, thinly sliced
1 tablespoon Tabasco sauce
1 teaspoon cayenne pepper
3 pounds mixed greens, rinsed and stemmed
1/2 cup chopped fresh flat-leaf parsley
Kosher salt and freshly ground black pepper
2 tablespoons filé powder

1. Heat the oil in a large soup pot over medium heat. Add the flour and cook, stirring constantly with a wooden spoon until deep golden brown, about 12 minutes. Add the onions, celery, bell pepper, and garlic and cook, stirring often, for 8 to 10 minutes.

2. Add 8 cups of water to the pot and stir to mix well. Add the Tabasco sauce and cayenne pepper and bring to a boil. Add the mixed greens, parsley, and salt and pepper to taste. Reduce the heat to medium-low and simmer, stirring occasionally, until the greens are very soft and the water is absorbed, about 1 hour. Stir in the filé powder. Taste and adjust the seasonings, if necessary.

Note: Filé powder or gumbo filé is made from dried and ground sassafras leaves. If it is not available in local markets, it can be ordered from specialty food and spice websites.

Bitter Greens Pizza
with Shallots and Havarti Cheese

Whether you serve this tasty pizza for a light supper, as a snack for hungry kids, or as a delicious nibble with cocktails it will be a huge hit. It's great with any mixed green, such as dandelion greens, kale, or spinach. You can make this with homemade pizza or with any good commercial dough.

makes 1 pizza, 4 to 6 servings

3 tablespoons olive oil

4 large shallots, finely chopped

1 pound Swiss chard, rinsed

$3/4$ to 1 pound mixed greens, rinsed and stemmed

Hot pepper flakes (optional)

Kosher salt

12 ounces pizza dough

4 to 6 ounces Havarti cheese, shredded

1. Preheat the oven to 350°F.

2. Heat the olive oil in a large sauté pan over low heat. Add the shallots and cook until soft, about 8 minutes.

3. Meanwhile, remove the Swiss chard stems from the leaves, chop coarsely, and add them to the shallots. Stack the chard leaves, roll them up lengthwise, and slice cross-wise into strips about $1/2$ inch wide. Chop the mixed greens. Add all of the greens with water still clinging to the leaves to the pan. The pan will be very full. Cook, covered, for a few minutes. Remove the lid and toss the greens with tongs to coat with the shallot mixture. When the greens are wilted, sprinkle with the hot pepper flakes, if using, and salt to taste. Cover and cook over medium-low heat, stirring occasionally, for about 8 minutes.

4. Cook the greens, uncovered, over low heat and simmer until all the moisture is gone. Remove from the heat and set aside.

5. Lightly oil a baking sheet or jelly-roll pan and press the pizza dough onto the pan about $1/4$-inch thick to form a 9 x 12-inch rectangle. Spread the greens mixture evenly over the dough. Sprinkle with the cheese. Bake for 12 to 15 minutes, until the dough is nicely browned. Let stand for 10 minutes, slide the pizza onto a cutting board, and slice with a pizza cutter.

Pan-Seared Salmon
with Braised Mixed Greens

Health food meets haute cuisine in this lovely pairing of salmon and braised mixed greens, such as Swiss chard, kale, collard, mustard, or dandelion greens. Salmon fillets cook evenly in a skillet when the skin is removed, so ask your fishmonger to cut the skin from the fillets when buying salmon for this dish. You can also do it yourself with a very sharp knife.

makes 4 servings

salmon:

1 tablespoon olive oil

4 (6-ounce) salmon fillets,
   skin removed

Kosher salt
   and freshly ground black pepper

greens:

2 tablespoons olive oil

1 small onion, chopped

1 garlic clove, chopped

2^1/$_2$ to 3 pounds mixed greens, rinsed,
   stemmed, and coarsely chopped

^{1}/$_4$ to ^{1}/$_2$ cup chicken or vegetable broth

^{1}/$_2$ cup chopped fresh flat-leaf parsley

^{1}/$_2$ cup chopped fresh cilantro

Lemon wedges, for garnish

1. To make the salmon, put the oil in a shallow baking dish. Add the salmon and turn to coat with the oil. Season to taste with salt and pepper and let sit for 30 minutes at room temperature.

2. To make the greens, heat the oil in a large skillet or sauté pan over medium heat. Add the onion and sauté until soft, about 5 minutes. Add the garlic and sauté for 1 minute. Add the greens and toss until they just begin to wilt. Add ^{1}/$_4$ cup of broth and sauté, tossing occasionally, until the greens are wilted and cooked through, 5 to 7 minutes. Add the parsley and cilantro and sauté for 1 minute. Add a bit more broth if the mixture seems dry. Cover and set aside.

3. Heat a large nonstick skillet over medium heat. Add the salmon fillets and cook for 3 minutes. Turn them over and cook for an additional 3 to 5 minutes, until opaque in the center.

4. Divide and arrange the greens in the center of four plates. Place 1 fillet over the center of the greens on each plate. Garnish with lemon wedges and serve at once.

Mixed greens are wilted by water, so wash and dry them just before using. You can either use a salad spinner or just a large bowl of cold water. Use the spinner or swirl the leaves around in the bowl of water to dislodge soil. Let the water settle so the soil gathers in the bottom of the bowl; change the water and repeat until the greens are clean. Then take the leaves out of the water and dry them with paper towels.

okra

Okra, a popular and important food worldwide, is a flowering tropical plant from the mallow family that is a native of West Africa. It is widely believed that it first reached this country during the days of slave trafficking.

Fresh okra is usually available year-round in the southern regions of this country, and from May to October in other areas. When selecting okra look for small tender pods that are bright green and unblemished. Pass on older pods that are dark or have dark spots. Although okra can be stored in the refrigerator for a day or two, it should be used shortly after picking or purchasing.

Okra may be an acquired taste to some because of its texture and gooiness. It is very popular all over the world and is used in a variety of native dishes like gumbos, soups, and stews. It can be served raw, added to salads, and pickled. Okra is good to sauté with other fresh vegetables like tomatoes and corn, and it is also excellent for deep-frying.

Okra Fritters

These fritters are very good to serve to people who "hate okra." Deep-frying reduces its mucilaginous quality, and they are quite delicious, especially when served with chutney for dipping. We like to use chickpea flour for these, but any all-purpose flour will work.

makes 4 to 6 servings

3/4 cup chickpea flour (see note), or unbleached flour

1 teaspoon dry mustard

1/2 teaspoon ground nutmeg

Kosher salt and freshly ground black pepper

2 large eggs

1/4 cup chopped fresh parsley

Vegetable oil, for frying

1 pound fresh young okra, rinsed, trimmed, and cut into 1/2-inch pieces

Apricot, peach, or plum chutney, for serving

1. Preheat the oven to 200°F. In a large, shallow bowl, whisk together the flour, dry mustard, nutmeg, and salt and pepper to taste. In a small, shallow bowl, beat the eggs and parsley together.

2. In a large, heavy saucepan or Dutch oven, heat 2 inches of oil until hot but not smoking, about 370°F on a candy thermometer.

3. Dip the okra into the egg mixture; then the flour mixture. Fry the okra in the hot oil, about 10 pieces at a time, until golden, about 4 minutes. Drain on paper towels. Sprinkle with salt to taste. Keep warm in the oven while frying the remaining okra. Serve at once with the chutney for dipping.

Note: Chickpea flour, also known as garbanzo bean flour or *besan*, can be purchased at Indian markets or health food stores.

Law and Okra

This recipe comes from actor Eric Bogosian's Grandma Lucy, and it is a version of the classic Armenian dish *bamiya*. We call it "Law and Okra" because he played Captain Danny Ross on the TV show *Law and Order*. This ragout of stewed okra and apricots is delicious no matter what you call it.

makes 4 servings

3 tablespoons olive oil

1 large onion, cut into $1/4$-inch slices

1 large garlic clove, thinly sliced

1 pound okra, rinsed and trimmed

8 to 10 dried apricots, halved

1 can (16 ounces) diced tomatoes, drained, juice reserved

Kosher salt and freshly ground pepper

1. Heat the oil in a large sauté pan over medium heat. Add the onion and sauté until translucent. Add the garlic and cook until fragrant. Add the okra and toss to coat. Add the apricots and tomatoes and stir to combine. Cover and simmer gently for about 10 minutes. Check every so often and if it seems dry, add a bit of the reserved tomato juice.

2. Remove the cover, add salt and pepper to taste, and cook until all of the liquid is absorbed and the okra is soft but not mushy. Serve at once.

Variation: This can be served as a main dish with lamb. Cut about $1/2$ pound of boneless lamb shoulder or lamb stew meat into $1/2$-inch pieces. Sauté the lamb in olive oil until it is nicely browned. Transfer to a separate bowl. Continue with the above recipe, and return the lamb to the pan when the okra is added. Add $1/2$ cup of the reserved tomato juice and cook for 10 minutes. Remove the cover and cook until the lamb is tender. Serve over rice.

Okra has antioxidants, is anti-inflammatory, and its mucilage soothes the intestines.

One-half cup of sliced okra (80g) has approximately:
calories 18
carbohydrates 3.9g
protein 1.5g
fat 0.2g

Of the recommended daily value, this portion provides:
vitamin A 5%
vitamin C 22%
vitamin E 1%
vitamin K 40%
vitamin B6 .... 7%
folate 9%
niacin 3%
pantothenic acid 2%
calcium 6%
iron 1%
magnesium 7%
manganese 12%
potassium 3%
phosphorous 3%
copper 3%

peas

Delicate and delicious fresh peas, also known as shell peas, are the seed pods of the legume *pisum sativum*. They most likely originated in the Mediterranean and parts of the Near East. Cousins to the shell pea are those peas with edible pods: snap peas and snow peas.

Fresh peas are a cool-weather crop and are at their very best in early spring. Look for peas that have bright, shiny pods that are well filled with peas. Pass on any that have dry or yellowish pods. Although fresh shell peas are best eaten immediately after picking or purchasing, they can be stored, unshelled, in the refrigerator for a day or two. Snap peas should be crisp and have a round, dark green pod that shows no sign of dryness or yellowing. Snow peas are lighter green and have a flat pod. They should also be fairly crisp and not limp. Snow peas and snap peas have a somewhat longer shelf life than shell peas and can be stored in the refrigerator, unwashed, in plastic bags for three to four days.

Garden-fresh peas are a seasonal treat and they can be served in so many wonderful ways. They're great to eat raw right from the shell or lightly steamed with a touch of butter and fresh mint. They're also fabulous in soups, or added to salads and other greens, rice, and pasta. Snap peas and snow peas are also excellent to eat raw and in salads, and they add gorgeous green color to all types of sautés and stir-fries.

Chilled Minted Pea Soup

If you grow shell peas, the common green peas in a pod, or if your local farmers' market sells them, use them for this light, easy soup. If not, frozen peas will work well. Be sure to strain the soup to rid it of the peas' skins, especially if the peas are frozen, since their skins tend to be a little tougher. Serve this lovely springtime soup laced with creamy yogurt and chopped fresh mint.

makes 6 servings

2 tablespoons olive oil

4 to 5 scallions (white and green parts), finely chopped

4 cups shelled fresh peas, or 2 packages (20 ounces) frozen peas, thawed

$1/4$ cup coarsely chopped fresh mint leaves

6 cups chicken or vegetable broth, preferably homemade

Kosher salt and freshly ground black pepper

$1/2$ cup half-and-half

Plain yogurt, for garnish

2 tablespoons minced fresh mint leaves, for garnish

1 scallion (white and green parts), thinly sliced, for garnish

1. In a large pot, heat the olive oil over medium-high heat. Add the scallions and cook, stirring, for 1 to 2 minutes, until softened. Add the peas and mint leaves and cook, stirring, for about 5 minutes, until softened and fragrant. Add the broth and bring to a boil over high heat. Reduce the heat and simmer for 15 to 20 minutes. Season to taste with salt and pepper. Let the soup cool to room temperature.

2. Transfer the soup in batches to a food processor or blender and process until smooth. Strain the mixture through a sieve into a pot, pushing hard with the back of a spoon to extract as much liquid as possible. You may also purée the soup using a food mill. Discard the solids.

3. Stir in the half-and-half and adjust the seasonings. Cover and refrigerate for at least 2 hours until chilled.

4. Stir well before ladling into chilled bowls. Garnish each serving with a dollop of yogurt, minced mint leaves, and sliced scallions.

Potato Salad with Peas and Mint

Fresh mint adds a cool, crisp flavor to potatoes and peas in this salad. You can use frozen baby peas in this dish if you don't have fresh.

makes 6 servings

2 pounds small red potatoes

1 cup shelled fresh peas or frozen baby peas, thawed

1 tablespoon Dijon mustard

1 tablespoon white wine vinegar

Kosher salt and freshly ground black pepper to taste

3 tablespoons olive oil

2 tablespoons chopped red onion

$\frac{1}{2}$ cup chopped fresh mint leaves

1. Put the potatoes in a large saucepan and cover with cold salted water. Bring to a boil and then reduce the heat to a simmer and cook, covered, until tender, about 15 minutes.

2. Meanwhile, combine the peas and $\frac{1}{4}$ cup of water in a small saucepan and simmer until just tender, about 3 minutes. Drain and set aside.

3. Whisk together the mustard, vinegar, and salt and pepper in a small bowl. Slowly add the olive oil and whisk until emulsified.

4. Drain the potatoes and cut into quarters. Place in a large serving bowl and add the vinaigrette. Toss to coat. Add the peas, onion, and mint and toss to combine. Taste and adjust the seasonings, if necessary, and serve.

Springtime Risi Bisi

Risi Bisi (Italian for Rice and Peas) is a beautiful risotto dish that features garden-fresh sweet peas. It should be soupy enough to serve in soup bowls, but thick enough to eat with a fork. If the rice seems sticky at the end of cooking, add a bit of hot broth or water so it's creamy. It's a terrific starter, or to serve as a main course, pair it with a simple arugula and sliced cherry tomato salad drizzled with oil and vinegar.

makes 8 first course or 6 main course servings

3 cups vegetable broth

3 cups water

¼ cup olive oil

2 garlic cloves, crushed

2 cups Arborio rice

½ cup dry white wine

2 cups shelled fresh peas

½ cup Parmesan cheese, plus more for the table

Kosher salt

1. Put the broth and water in a large saucepan on the back burner and bring to a gentle simmer.

2. In a heavy 2-quart saucepan, heat the olive oil. Add the garlic cloves and cook just until they start to brown. Remove the garlic and set aside. Add the rice and stir to coat with the oil. Continue to cook and stir for 2 minutes. Add the wine and continue to stir until it is absorbed. Add the hot broth ½ cup at a time, allowing each addition to be absorbed before adding the next and stirring after each addition.

3. When you have used up half the broth, stir in the peas. When you have used up three-quarters of the broth, check the texture of the rice. It should be soft but not mushy. If the rice needs to cook longer add more water to the broth pot, then add to the rice and cook, stirring, until desired doneness.

4. Stir in the cheese and season with salt to taste. Serve in shallow soup bowls with additional cheese.

Peas and Onions Nonnie-Style

Low and slow is the way to go when cooking this sweet, creamy side dish. Keep an eye on it as it simmers to make sure it doesn't burn, or the peas will get hard. This dish comes from Liz's grandmother, or Nonnie, and she always served it with mashed potatoes.

makes 6 servings

2 tablespoons butter

3 tablespoons olive oil

2 small yellow onions, thinly sliced

1$\frac{1}{2}$ pounds fresh peas, shelled,
  or 2 packages (10 ounces) frozen peas, thawed

Kosher salt and freshly ground black pepper

In a medium sauté pan, heat the butter and olive oil over low heat. Add the onions and cook slowly for 30 minutes, stirring occasionally. Add the peas and cook over very low heat for an additional 30 minutes, until the peas begin to brown slightly. Season with salt and pepper to taste and serve immediately.

Consumption of green peas improves the health of bones and arteries. The nutrients in green peas support the energy-producing cells and system of the body, providing a natural pick-up. Fresh green peas provide a little more nutrition and antioxidants than dried peas.

One cup of boiled peas has approximately:

calories	134
carbohydrates	25g
protein	8.6g
fat	0.4g

Of the recommended daily value, this portion provides:

vitamin A	26%
vitamin C	38%
vitamin E	1%
vitamin K	52%
vitamin B6	17%
folate	25%
niacin	16%
pantothenic acid	2%
calcium	4%
iron	14%
magnesium	16%
manganese	42%
potassium	12%
phosphorous	19%
copper	14%
selenium	4%

Sautéed Peas, Kale, and Chorizo

The robust combination of garlicky green peas and kale and smoky chopped chorizo is wonderful with egg dishes or roast chicken.

makes 4 to 6 servings

2 tablespoons olive oil

1 garlic clove, thinly sliced

3 scallions, minced

2 cups shelled fresh peas,
 or 1 package (10 ounces) frozen peas, thawed

1/4 cup white wine

3 cups chopped fresh kale

1/4 cup finely chopped chorizo

Kosher salt and freshly ground black pepper

In a large skillet or sauté pan, heat the olive oil over medium heat. Add the garlic and scallions and cook until softened, about 2 minutes. Add the peas and sauté for 2 minutes. Add the wine, bring to a boil, and simmer for 1 minute. Add the kale and cook, stirring and shaking the pan, until wilted. Add the chorizo and salt and pepper to taste and cook for 1 minute longer. Serve at once.

Creamy Linguine
with Fresh Peas and Pancetta

This is a fantastic pasta dish that makes the most of springtime peas.

makes 6 first course or 4 main course servings
1/2 pound thinly sliced pancetta
1 pound linguine
1 1/2 cups shelled fresh peas
2 tablespoons olive oil
1 tablespoon finely chopped garlic
1/2 cup chopped shallots
1 cup heavy cream
1/2 cup freshly grated Parmesan cheese, plus more for serving
Kosher salt and freshly ground black pepper
Zest of 1/2 lemon, finely minced

1. Chop the pancetta into 1/2-inch pieces. Sauté in a skillet over medium-low heat until just crisp, 10 minutes. Drain on paper towels and set aside.

2. Cook the linguine in a large pot of boiling salted water until just tender. Drain but do not rinse.

3. Meanwhile, bring a saucepan of salted water to a boil. Add the peas and boil until just tender, 2 to 4 minutes. Drain and rinse immediately under cold water. Drain well and set aside.

4. In a skillet large enough to hold the cooked pasta, heat the olive oil over medium heat and sauté the garlic and shallots until softened. Add the cream, reduce the heat to low, and cook until thickened, about 5 minutes.

5. Return the heat to medium, add the peas to the sauce, and bring to a low simmer. Add the linguine and pancetta and toss to coat well. Add the cheese, salt and pepper to taste, and the lemon zest, and toss well. Serve immediately with additional grated cheese.

Sautéed Snap Peas with Honey and Mint

Honey and mint add a surprisingly wonderful taste to fresh cooked snap peas. This is an excellent dish to serve with grilled fish, shrimp, or chicken.

makes 6 servings
2 tablespoons olive oil
2 tablespoons chopped shallots
1 pound fresh sugar snap peas, trimmed
1 tablespoon rice vinegar
1 teaspoon honey
2 tablespoons finely chopped fresh mint leaves
Kosher salt and freshly ground black pepper

Heat the olive oil over medium heat in a large skillet. Add the shallots and cook until softened, about 2 minutes. Add the snap peas and cook for 3 minutes. Add the vinegar and honey and cook, stirring, for 2 minutes. Add the mint and salt and pepper to taste, stir, and serve at once.

Snap and snow peas in their edible pods assist in bone and cardiovascular health.

One cup of fresh snap or snow peas has approximately:
calories 41
carbohydrates................................. 7.4g
protein 2.7g
fat 0.2g

Of the recommended daily value, this portion provides:
vitamin A....................................... 21%
vitamin C...98%
vitamin E..2%

vitamin K... 31%
vitamin B6..8%
folate 10%
niacin 3%
pantothenic acid 7%
calcium 4%
iron 11%
magnesium 6%
manganese 12%
potassium 6%
phosphorous....................................5%
copper..4%
selenium 1%

Sautéed Snap Peas, Sweet Corn, and Red Peppers

Nothing could be simpler or better than this summery dish of fresh and crunchy snap peas tossed together with corn and red peppers.

makes 4 to 6 servings

$1/2$ pound fresh sugar snap peas, trimmed

1 red bell pepper, cored, seeded, and cut into thin 1 1/2-inch strips

2 tablespoons olive oil

2 cups fresh corn kernels

$1/3$ cup chopped scallions

Kosher salt and freshly ground black pepper

2 tablespoons chopped fresh chives

1. Bring a pot of salted water to a boil. Add the peas and red pepper strips and simmer for 2 minutes. Drain and rinse in a colander under cold water and set aside.

2. Heat the olive oil over medium heat in a large skillet. Add the corn, scallions, snap peas, red pepper strips, and salt and pepper to taste. Cook, shaking and stirring the skillet, for about 2 minutes. Add the chives, stir, and serve at once.

Ginger-Orange Snap Peas

Quickly cooked fresh snap peas with an added dash of fresh ginger and orange zest are a delightful springtime side dish. Snow peas may be substituted in this recipe.

makes 6 servings

1 pound fresh sugar snap peas, trimmed

1 teaspoon rice vinegar

2 tablespoons extra-virgin olive oil

2 teaspoons grated orange zest

1 tablespoon finely grated ginger

Kosher salt and freshly ground black pepper

1. Bring a large pot of salted water to a boil. Add the snap peas and cook until crisp-tender, about 2 minutes. Drain and transfer to a large bowl.

2. In a small bowl, whisk together the vinegar, olive oil, orange zest, and ginger. Pour over the snap peas and toss to combine. Season to taste with salt and pepper. Serve warm, cold, or at room temperature.

Snow Pea Salad with Walnut Vinaigrette

For spring gardeners, gracefully shaped snow peas are an early reward. For shoppers, fresh, local snow peas are easily available. Cook them very quickly, rinsing them under cold, running water to help them retain their bright color and crisp snap. Try to make this salad no longer than an hour or two before serving. It's best when served fresh.

makes 6 servings

$1^1/_2$ pounds fresh snow peas

2 tablespoons fresh lime juice

1 tablespoon light soy sauce

$^1/_2$ cup walnut oil

6 scallions (white and green parts), thinly sliced on the diagonal

2 teaspoons sliced fresh ginger

$^1/_2$ cup coarsely chopped, lightly toasted walnuts (see Note)

1. Snap off the stems of the snow peas and remove the strings. Blanch the snow peas in enough boiling water to cover for about 1 minute until they turn bright green. Drain immediately and rinse with cold water to stop the cooking. Drain and set aside.

2. Whisk the lime juice and soy sauce together in a small bowl. Slowly add the walnut oil, whisking constantly, until the vinaigrette thickens.

3. Put the snow peas in a serving bowl and add the scallions, ginger, and walnuts. Toss with the vinaigrette. Serve at once.

Note: To toast the walnuts, spread them on a baking sheet and toast them in a preheated 350ºF oven for about 5 minutes until golden brown. Shake the pan once or twice for even toasting. Slide the nuts off the baking sheet as soon as they reach the desired color to stop the cooking and let them cool.

Spicy Shrimp and Snow Pea Stir-Fry

This shrimp dish is hot! hot! hot! And it's very good, too. The heat comes from a Southeast Asian chile paste that is known as sambal oelek. It can be found in Asian markets or the international sections of most supermarkets.

makes 4 servings

sauce:

1 tablespoon tomato paste

1 teaspoon chile paste (sambal oelek)

2 teaspoons cider vinegar

1 teaspoon sugar

1 teaspoon sesame oil

Kosher salt and freshly ground black pepper

1 tablespoon peanut oil

1 tablespoon minced fresh ginger

1 garlic clove, thinly sliced

3 scallions, trimmed and finely chopped, divided

1 pound large fresh shrimp, shelled and deveined

2 cups fresh snow peas (about $1/2$ pound), trimmed

1 teaspoon soy sauce

$1/2$ cup chopped fresh cilantro sprigs, for garnish (optional)

1. To make the sauce, in a small bowl, whisk together the tomato paste, chile paste, vinegar, sugar, sesame oil, and salt and pepper to taste. Set aside.

2. Heat a wok or a large sauté pan over high heat. Add the peanut oil and heat until just smoking. Stir-fry the ginger, garlic, and 2 of the scallions for 20 seconds. Add the shrimp and stir-fry for 1 minute. Add the snow peas and soy sauce and stir-fry for 1 minute.

3. Add the sauce and continue to stir-fry over high heat until the shrimp and snow peas are cooked through, about 3 minutes. Transfer to a serving bowl or platter, garnish with the remaining scallion and the cilantro, if desired, and serve at once.

They are called snow peas because they can grow at the end of winter, just before the last spring freeze and can still keep growing well even when covered with snow.

Snow peas host beneficial bacteria, rhizobia, that fix nitrogen in the soil, so it is a useful companion plant with all green, leafy vegetables that benefit from high nitrogen content in their soil.

Snow peas are nutritious and filling, yet not as high in total carbohydrates and fats as normal peas.

Snap peas differ from snow peas in that their pods are round as opposed to flat.

A great thing to do with snap peas is to slow roast them: Toss the whole pods in a little olive oil and salt, and spread them out on a baking sheet. Roast in the oven at 300°F, tossing every 10 minutes or so until they begin to brown and carmelize, about 20 to 30 minutes. Serve at room temperature alongside any roast meat.

peppers

All members of the pepper family, sweet or hot, are members of the capsicum family. Sweet peppers are referred to as "bells" because of their shape, and hot peppers are known as chile peppers because of their heat. They originated in South America.

Although peppers are available all year, they are at their freshest and best in the late summer and early fall months. Look for peppers that have vibrant colors and green, fresh-looking stems. They should also be fairly heavy and firm to the touch. Avoid any that have soft spots or blemishes on their skins. Peppers can be stored, unwashed, in the refrigerator, for up to a week.

Peppers are very versatile and there are no hard and fast rules for preparing them. They are good when eaten raw, sautéed, grilled, fried, or stuffed, and they are essential additions to salads, soups, and stews.

Grilled Eggplant and Peppers

Grilled eggplant and peppers are very tasty served on their own, or as a side dish with grilled fish or lamb. They're also excellent tucked into a sandwich on a warm baguette with a slice of cheese and a drizzle of good olive oil.

makes 6 servings
$1/4$ cup olive oil
1 garlic clove, thinly sliced
Kosher salt and freshly ground black pepper
1 large eggplant, sliced into $1/4$-inch-thick rounds
2 large green bell peppers, stemmed, seeded, and quartered
Extra-virgin olive oil, for serving

1. Whisk the oil, garlic, and salt and pepper to taste together in a small bowl. Brush the eggplant and peppers with the mixture.

2. Prepare a gas or charcoal grill. When the fire is medium-hot and the coals are covered with a light coating of ash and glow deep red, put the eggplant on the grill and cook for about 3 minutes per side, until golden brown. After about 2 minutes, add the peppers and cook until lightly charred, about 2 minutes per side.

3. Drizzle the eggplant and peppers with a bit of olive oil and additional salt and pepper and serve warm or at room temperature.

Sweet and Sour Peppers

This is a gorgeous, glossy side dish to serve with fish or chicken.

makes 6 servings
6 large green bell peppers
1 stick (¼ pound) butter
¼ cup cider vinegar
¼ cup water
2 tablespoons sugar
Kosher salt

1. Wash, trim, and cut the peppers into 1-inch strips.

2. Melt the butter in a large sauté pan over medium heat. Add the peppers and toss to coat. Cook for 10 minutes, tossing often, being careful not to burn the butter. Add the vinegar and water, cover the pan, and simmer over low heat for 10 minutes. Remove the lid, turn the heat back to medium, and sprinkle the sugar over the peppers. Cook, stirring constantly, until the sugar is melted and the sauce begins to thicken and caramelize. Season to taste with salt. Transfer to a serving dish and serve at once.

Bell peppers are low in saturated fat, cholesterol, and sodium and high in dietary fiber. The antioxidants in bell peppers neutralize free radicals that roam the body and damage cells.

One cup of boiled bell pepper has approximately:
calories 39
carbohydrates................................. 9g
protein 5.3g
fat 0.3g

Of the recommended daily value, this portion provides:
vitamin A.. 13%
vitamin C..................................... 167%
vitamin E.. 3%
vitamin K....................................... 17%

vitamin B6..................................... 16%
folate 5%
niacin 3%
pantothenic acid 1%
calcium 1%
iron 3%
magnesium 3%
manganese 8%
potassium 6%
phosphorous................................... 2%
copper... 4%
selenium 1%

Stuffed Peppers with Zucchini

While this dish won't make much of a dent in your end-of-summer zucchini crop, these stuffed peppers make a lovely light meal or side dish. Steaming the peppers first is necessary to insure that they are completely cooked when served.

makes 6 servings

3 tablespoons olive oil

3 tablespoons unsalted butter

1 large yellow onion, chopped

4 cups shredded zucchini

$\frac{1}{2}$ cup freshly grated Pecorino Romano cheese

4 cups seasoned dry bread stuffing mix or fresh breadcrumbs

Vegetable or chicken broth, or water

3 medium green bell peppers

6 ounces fontina cheese

1. In a large sauté pan, heat the olive oil and butter over low heat. Add the onion and cook until very soft and caramelized, about 30 minutes. Add the shredded zucchini. Turn up the heat slightly and cook, stirring occasionally, for about 30 minutes more. The zucchini will give off a good amount of liquid, but don't let them dry out. When the mixture is very soft and creamy, remove from the heat and add the Pecorino Romano cheese and the bread stuffing and mix until it is well combined. If the mixture seems dry, add a bit of broth or water.

2. Meanwhile, preheat the oven to 350°F. Cut the peppers in half lengthwise and remove stems, seeds, and white pith from the inside of each pepper half. Put the peppers in a steamer basket and steam for 10 minutes. Remove and let cool a bit. Arrange the peppers, cut side up, in a baking dish or casserole.

3. Spoon the zucchini mixture into each pepper half. Slice the fontina cheese into $\frac{1}{8}$-inch pieces and cover the tops of each pepper with slices of cheese. Bake, uncovered, until the cheese is soft and melted, about 30 minutes.

Peppers with Chicken Livers, Tomatoes, and Onions

The key to making this savory dish is to not overcook the livers or they will become dry. This makes a warm and tasty winter supper.

makes 6 servings

2 tablespoons butter

3 tablespoons olive oil

4 large green bell peppers, cut into $1/2$-inch strips

2 large yellow onions, cut into $1/2$-inch-thick slices

1 pound chicken livers, drained and patted dry

1 can (16 ounces) stewed tomatoes

Kosher salt and freshly ground black pepper

Brown rice or egg noodles, for serving

1. In a large sauté pan with a lid, heat the butter and olive oil over medium heat. Add the peppers and onions and cook, stirring, for about 10 minutes, until softened.

2. Push the vegetables to the side of the pan and add the chicken livers. Cook for 2 minutes, then turn them over and cook an additional 2 minutes. Add the stewed tomatoes and stir together. Cover the pan and simmer gently for 15 minutes or until the livers are done. Serve with rice or egg noodles.

salad greens

Mild Greens

Bibb Lettuce: Soft, small heads with large, pale green outer leaves and a sweet, mild taste.

Boston Lettuce: Fluffy, loose heads with soft, pale green leaves. Pale green and red varieties.

Iceberg Lettuce: Compact, crisp heads with very pale green leaves.

Loose Leaf Lettuce: Includes a wide variety such as green leaf, red leaf, and oak leaf. Large, soft medium green or red leaves.

Mache: Light or deep green. Delicate, sweet and nutty flavor.

Romaine Lettuce: Large head with long, crisp, green or red leaves and a rather sweet flavor.

Spinach: Deep green, heart-shaped leaves, crisp if large and tender if small. Fresh flat-leaved varieties have a more intense flavor.

Peppery Greens

Arugula: Dark green, elongated leaves with a rich, mildly peppery flavor. Also known as *rocket* or *rucula*.

Mizuna: Dark green, feathery leaves with a mild peppery flavor. Among the best known Asian greens in the U.S.

Mustard Greens: Green mustard and purple varieties with an intense peppery taste. It is the most strongly flavored of Asian greens.

Watercress: Dark green, glossy leaves on tender, leggy stems with a spicy flavor.

Bitter Greens

Belgian Endive: Whitish, yellow, narrow, cup-shaped leaves with bittersweet flavor.

Chicory: Narrow, twisted, frilly leaves that are dark green at the top and very light green at the stem. The leaves have a pronounced but pleasant bitterness. The outer leaves are tough and more bitter.

Escarole: Cut-edged leaves that are dark green at the top and lighter green at the stem. The inner, light-colored leaves have a nutty flavor.

Frisée: Small, tender, curly leaves with a white center. Mildly bitter, but somewhat delicate flavor.

Radicchio: Reddish-purple leaves in a small tight head that resembles a small cabbage. It has a pleasant, bitter flavor.

scallions

Scallions, also known as green onions or spring onions, are members of the allium or onion family. They are young onions that are harvested before their bulbs mature. They most likely originated in the Mediterranean.

Scallions are a hardy plant and they are readily available year-round. Look for scallions with crisp and bright green stalks and that show no signs of yellowing. They will keep in a plastic bag, unwashed, in the refrigerator for up to a week.

Scallions have an assertive yet delicate flavor that is similar to that of the leek. Although they are usually thought of as just an addition or garnish to many dishes, we like to use them as the main tasty ingredient in pancakes and vegetable roasts, or to cook on the grill.

Scallion Pancakes with Soy Dipping Sauce

The delicate flavor of scallions shines through in these bite-size pancakes. They cook very quickly in hot oil, so make the dipping sauce in advance and have hot sauce or Sriracha sauce on hand to serve with them. These are fun to make for friends when they're hanging out in the kitchen having cocktails.

makes about 2 dozen pancakes

soy dipping sauce:
2 tablespoons chicken broth
2 tablespoons soy sauce
1 tablespoon minced scallions
1 teaspoon hot sauce

scallion pancakes:
3 bunches scallions, trimmed, divided
2 eggs
1 tablespoon soy sauce
$\frac{1}{2}$ cup chopped fresh flat-leaf parsley
1 cup unbleached flour
Peanut or canola oil, for frying

1. To make the dipping sauce, in a small bowl, whisk together the broth, soy sauce, scallions, and hot sauce and set aside.

2. To make the pancakes, bring a medium pot of salted water to a boil. Coarsely chop 2 bunches of the scallions and add to the water. Cook until tender, about 5 minutes. Meanwhile, mince the remaining bunch of scallions and set aside.

3. Drain the cooked scallions and reserve a bit of the cooking liquid. Transfer the scallions to a blender and purée until very smooth, adding some of the cooking liquid, if necessary.

4. In a medium bowl, whisk the scallion purée, the eggs, soy sauce, parsley, and reserved minced scallions together. Gently stir in the flour until well blended. Coat the bottom of a nonstick skillet with oil over medium-high heat. Drop the batter into the pan with a tablespoon and flatten a bit with the bottom of the spoon. Cook until lightly browned, about 2 minutes on each side. Set aside on paper towels. Serve at once with the soy dipping sauce and hot sauce or Sriracha sauce.

Grilled Scallions

Grilled scallions are a terrific accompaniment to hamburgers, hot dogs, or any grilled meat.

makes 6 servings

12 scallions

Olive oil, for brushing

Kosher salt

1 tablespoon balsamic vinegar

1 teaspoon sugar

1. Prepare a medium-hot gas or charcoal grill. Brush each scallion with olive oil, sprinkle with salt to taste, and grill just until they start to soften and brown. Remove from the grill to a cutting board and slice crosswise into 2-inch pieces.

2. In a bowl, whisk together the vinegar and sugar. Add the scallions and toss well. Serve at once.

spinach

Spinach is one of the healthiest vegetables around and also one of the simplest to cook. It is said that spinach originally comes from Southwest Asia, most likely Persia. It was introduced to Spain in the eleventh century and its cultivation spread throughout Europe.

It is now grown all over the world except in tropical regions. Fresh spinach is available in markets year-round. When selecting spinach, look for crisp, dark-green leaves that show no sign of wilting or yellowing. If you must buy bagged spinach, sort through it and get rid of any yellowing or wet leaves. Store spinach, unwashed, in a plastic bag in the refrigerator for up to three days.

Spinach is a flavorful green with deep, rich flavor. It is wonderful in soups and salads and it combines well with other leafy greens. It's a fantastic side dish when simply sautéed with olive oil and garlic or stirred into a cream sauce. And whether stuffed into ravioli or shaped into dumplings, it works beautifully as a pasta dish. Just don't overcook it!

Spinach and Arugula Soup

This smooth and versatile soup is lovely to serve warm in the fall or winter or chilled in the warmer months.

makes 4 servings

4 tablespoons ($^1/_2$ stick) unsalted butter

2 shallots, thinly sliced

3 scallions, trimmed and minced

2 cups peeled and chopped potatoes

Kosher salt and freshly ground pepper

2 cups chicken broth, divided

2 cups fresh spinach, rinsed, stemmed, and coarsely chopped

1 cup arugula leaves, rinsed, stemmed, and coarsely chopped

Crème fraîche, for garnish

Minced fresh chives, for garnish

1. In a large soup pot, heat the butter over medium heat. Add the shallots and scallions and sauté until wilted, about 5 minutes. Add the potatoes, salt and pepper to taste, and 1 cup of the broth. Cover and simmer over low heat for 10 minutes. Add the spinach and arugula and simmer, stirring occasionally, until the potatoes are fork-tender, about 10 minutes. Set aside and let cool. Transfer to a food processor and blend until smooth.

2. Return the mixture to the pot. Add the remaining 1 cup of broth, blend well, and simmer until the soup is heated through. Taste and adjust the seasonings. Ladle into soup bowls, garnish with a spoonful of crème fraîche and a sprinkle of chives, and serve at once. To serve the soup cold, chill in the refrigerator for 4 hours or overnight.

Spinach, Bacon, and Tomato Salad

This scrumptious salad is especially delicious with garden-fresh spinach and cherry tomatoes and it makes a very satisfying summer lunch.

makes 6 servings
dressing:
¼ cup mayonnaise
1 tablespoon white vinegar
1 tablespoon fresh lemon juice
¼ cup buttermilk
3 tablespoons crumbled Gorgonzola cheese
Kosher salt and freshly ground black pepper

salad:
3 slices thick-cut bacon
2 tablespoons olive oil
1 cup ½-inch bread cubes
6 cups (about 1½ pounds) fresh spinach
½ red onion, thinly sliced
½ cup red and yellow cherry tomatoes, halved,
   or 1 large ripe tomato, cut into ½-inch pieces

1. To make the dressing, in a small bowl, whisk the mayonnaise, vinegar, and lemon juice together. Add the buttermilk and whisk again. Stir in the cheese and season to taste with salt and pepper. Taste and adjust the seasonings, if necessary. (The dressing will keep, covered, in the refrigerator for up to 1 day.)

2. To make the salad, fry the bacon in a skillet until crisp and drain on paper towels. When cool enough to handle, crumble and set aside.

3. Wipe out the pan with paper towels. Heat the olive oil in the pan over medium heat. Add the bread cubes and cook, stirring often, until lightly browned, 7 to 8 minutes. Drain on paper towels.

4. Combine the spinach, onion, and half of the croutons in a large shallow bowl and toss together. Pour half of the dressing over the salad and gently toss. Arrange the bacon, tomatoes, and remaining croutons over the salad and drizzle with the remaining dressing. Add a bit more pepper, if desired, and serve.

Sautéed Spinach
with Garlic, Ginger, and Chiles

Fresh garlic, ginger, and chilies add a lively zing to just about everything, and this simple sautéed spinach is no exception.

makes 4 to 6 servings

1 tablespoon sesame oil

1 tablespoon olive oil

1 tablespoon minced garlic

2 tablespoons minced ginger

1 teaspoon minced fresh chile pepper
(such as jalapeño or ancho), or $1/2$ teaspoon red pepper flakes

1 pound fresh spinach, rinsed and stemmed

Kosher salt and freshly ground black pepper

1. In a large sauté pan, heat the oils over medium-high heat until hot but not smoking. Add the garlic, ginger, and chile pepper and sauté, stirring, for about 15 seconds.

2. Add the spinach and cook, stirring constantly, until it is just wilted, about 2 minutes. Remove from the heat, season with salt and pepper to taste, and serve at once.

Chilled Sesame Spinach

This recipe is so easy, refreshing, and delicious; you may want to double it. Use the freshest spinach you can find.

makes 4 servings

1$^1/_2$ pounds fresh spinach, rinsed and stemmed

2 tablespoons soy sauce

1 tablespoon white vinegar

1 tablespoon sesame oil

1 tablespoon minced fresh ginger

1 tablespoon sugar

$^1/_2$ teaspoon red pepper flakes

1. Fill a large bowl with ice and cold water.

2. Bring a large pot of salted water to a boil over high heat. Add the spinach and cook for 1 minute. Drain the spinach and transfer to the cold water to stop the cooking.

3. Drain the spinach again and squeeze as much moisture as possible out with paper towels or a kitchen towel. Chop coarsely and transfer to a bowl.

4. In a small bowl, whisk the soy sauce, vinegar, sesame oil, ginger, sugar, and red pepper flakes together.

5. Pour the dressing over the spinach and toss well with a fork to coat the spinach. Chill the spinach for a few hours before serving.

Creamed Spinach

Most people go to steak houses for the steak, but we go mainly for the creamed spinach. We have no idea why it became a side dish to accompany huge slabs of grilled meat, but it is terrific with everything.

makes 6 servings

3 pounds baby spinach, rinsed and stemmed

2 tablespoons unsalted butter

1 onion, finely chopped

2 tablespoons unbleached all-purpose flour

1 cup warm whole milk

$3/4$ cup freshly grated Parmesan cheese, divided

$1/4$ teaspoon ground nutmeg

Kosher salt and freshly ground black pepper

1. Preheat the oven to 350°F. Butter a gratin or baking dish.

2. Heat 1 inch of salted water in a large pot. Add the spinach, cover and cook, stirring occasionally, until wilted, about 2 minutes. Drain in a colander and rinse under cold running water until cool. Squeeze out as much moisture as possible. Coarsely chop the spinach and transfer to a large bowl.

3. Heat the butter in a small, heavy-bottomed saucepan over low heat. Add the onion and cook, stirring occasionally, until softened, about 5 minutes. Whisk in the flour and cook, stirring, for 2 minutes. Slowly add the milk, whisking constantly, until thickened, 3 to 5 minutes. Whisk in $1/2$ cup of the cheese, the nutmeg, and salt and pepper to taste. Add the cream sauce to the spinach and mix thoroughly. Taste and adjust the seasonings, if necessary.

4. Spoon the spinach into the prepared baking dish. (The spinach may be prepared up to this point and will keep, covered, in the refrigerator, for a day. Bring to room temperature before baking.)

5. Sprinkle the remaining $1/4$ cup cheese over the top of the spinach and bake for 15 minutes. Serve at once.

Spinach has a high nutritional value and is extremely rich in antioxidants, especially when fresh, steamed, or quickly boiled.

One cup of boiled spinach has approximately:

calories	41
carbohydrates	6.7g
protein	2.7g
fat	0.5g

Of the recommended daily value, this portion provides:

vitamin A	377%
vitamin C	29%
vitamin E	3.7%
vitamin K	11%
vitamin B6	22%
folate	66%
niacin	4%
pantothenic acid	3%
calcium	24%
iron	36%
magnesium	39%
manganese	84%
potassium	24%
phosphorous	10%
copper	16%
selenium	4%

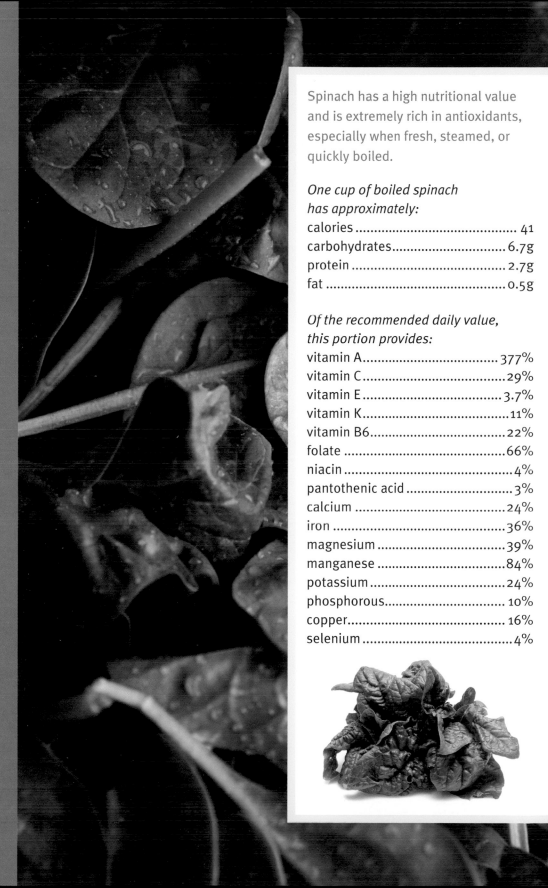

Spinach and Tofu Saag Paneer

Saag Paneer is a traditional Indian dish that uses ghee (clarified butter) and Indian curd cheese (paneer). We adapted this totally vegan recipe from our friends at Candle Café, New York City's premiere vegetarian restaurant. It's very tasty indeed.

makes 6 servings

2 blocks (about 12 ounces) firm tofu

4 tablespoons olive oil, divided

1 tablespoon turmeric

2 teaspoons cumin

2 teaspoons coriander

1 teaspoon chili powder

Kosher salt

1 tablespoon minced garlic

1 tablespoon minced fresh ginger

1 jalapeño pepper, seeded and minced

2 pounds fresh spinach, rinsed and stemmed

1. Preheat the oven to 350°F.

2. Drain the tofu, pat dry, and cut into 3/4-inch cubes. Put in a large bowl.

3. Whisk together 2 tablespoons of the olive oil, the turmeric, cumin, coriander, chili powder, and salt to taste. Pour over the tofu and toss to coat. Arrange the cubes in a single layer on a baking sheet and bake until crisp and puffy, about 20 minutes.

4. Heat the remaining 2 tablespoons of oil in a large skillet over medium heat. Add the garlic, ginger, and jalapeño and sauté for 2 minutes. Add the spinach and sauté until the spinach is wilted, about 5 minutes. Add the tofu and sauté for 5 minutes. Add salt to taste and serve at once.

Spinach, Swiss Chard, and Feta Cheese Pie

Here's a fantastic dish to serve as a side or on its own. It's also good to cut into very small squares and serve as an appetizer.

makes 6 to 8 servings

2 tablespoons olive oil, divided

2 pounds fresh spinach, rinsed and stemmed

1 pound Swiss chard, rinsed and stemmed

6 eggs

1 cup (about 4 ounces) crumbled feta cheese

3/4 cup freshly grated Parmesan cheese, divided

Freshly ground black pepper

2 tablespoons pine nuts or chopped walnuts

1. Preheat the oven to 375°F. Coat a 2-quart baking dish with 1 tablespoon of the olive oil.

2. Fill a large pot with water and bring to a boil. Add the spinach and Swiss chard and cook until wilted, about 1 minute. Drain and let cool. Squeeze out as much liquid as possible and coarsely chop.

3. In a large bowl, whisk the eggs with the feta, 1/2 cup of the Parmesan cheese, and the pepper to taste. Stir in the spinach and chard and the pine nuts and mix thoroughly. Spoon the mixture into the baking dish and smooth out. Sprinkle the remaining 1/4 cup Parmesan cheese on top. Drizzle the remaining 1 tablespoon olive oil over the pie and bake until golden and sizzling, 35 to 40 minutes. Let cool for about 5 minutes before serving.

Note: The pie can be baked and refrigerated up to a day ahead of time. Bring to room temperature before reheating.

Spinach Malfatti with Sage Butter Sauce

Creamy Spinach Malfatti is a wonderful first course to serve on Christmas Eve. Although making these can be a bit of a process, if you make the dumpling mixture the day before, and with kitchen helpers, you can have a fun day of dumpling making.

makes 6 to 8 servings

dumplings:

2 (10-ounce) packages fresh spinach

2 cups ricotta cheese

²⁄₃ cup freshly grated Parmesan cheese, plus more for serving

1 tablespoon salt

1 egg, beaten

2 tablespoons butter, melted

½ cup flour, plus more for shaping

sage butter sauce:

1 stick (¼ pound) butter

2 tablespoons torn fresh sage leaves, or 1 tablespoon dried

1 tablespoon Frangelico liqueur

Kosher salt and freshly ground black pepper

1. To make the dumplings, wash the spinach in several changes of cold water and drain. Bring a large pot of salted water to a boil and blanch the spinach for 2 minutes. Drain and rinse and drain again for about 30 minutes; then spread the spinach leaves out in a single layer on a clean dish towel. Place another towel on top, roll it up, and wring it out over the sink to get out as much water as you can. Chop the spinach finely and transfer to a large bowl.

2. Add the ricotta and Parmesan cheeses, salt, egg, and melted butter to the spinach and stir until well blended. Gradually add in the flour, mixing after each addition until the mixture is well combined and forms a dough. Refrigerate for up to 2 hours or overnight.

3. Line a baking sheet with waxed paper. Put about 1½ teaspoons of flour into a large wine glass. Drop 1 teaspoon of the cheese mixture into the glass and swirl it around until it forms a torpedo-shaped dumpling about 1 inch long (this takes a little practice, but you'll get the hang of it). Remove the dumpling carefully to the baking sheet. Continue with the remaining mixture, adding more flour to the glass as needed.

4. Fill a pot with 2 inches of water and bring to a boil. Drop the dumplings into the boiling water, about 10 at a time, and boil for 2 minutes. Remove with a slotted spoon to a colander and keep warm. Continue with the rest of the dumplings.

5. Meanwhile, to make the sage butter sauce, melt the butter in a saucepan and stir in the sage leaves. Add the Frangelico and salt and pepper to taste and stir over low heat.

6. Remove the dumplings to a large, flat serving bowl. Pour the sauce over the dumplings and toss very gently so they are well coated. Serve at once with Parmesan cheese.

swiss chard

Another common name for Swiss chard, "leaf beet," better describes its botanical origins. Chard is really a beet top that went wild in the garden. Early vegetable lovers thought it was a cardoon, or *chardon,* and it has been called Swiss chard ever since.

There are several varieties of Swiss chard with leaves in a range of greens and stalks varying from white to pink to red to bright orange. It has a relatively long growing season, usually June through October. Because it needs very little attention and is a prolific grower, tolerates poor soil, and withstands frost and freezes, it is truly a gardener's dream. Look for bunches that have fresh green leaves and pass up any that are yellow or discolored.

Since Swiss chard is fairly perishable, keep refrigerator storage time to a minimum. Store the greens, unwashed, in the refrigerator for up to three days. If the stalks are separated from the leaves they can be stored a day or two longer.

This gorgeous green, with its mildly earthy and slightly bitter flavor can be prepared in a number of ways—quickly sautéed in olive oil with a splash of fresh lemon juice, baked into a savory tart or pasta dish, or stirred into a creamy soup to enhance its flavor.

Any way this versatile vegetable is used, it is simply delectable. The following recipes will have you seeking out the best and freshest bunches of Swiss chard to cook and savor in many different and delicious ways.

Swiss Chard and Sopressata Crostini

Here's a nice appetizer to make while the grill is hot—slices of grilled baguette topped with sopressata, sautéed Swiss chard, and a sprinkling of cheese.

makes 6 to 8 servings

1 baguette or loaf of ciabatta bread, cut on the diagonal into $1/2$-inch slices

2 tablespoons olive oil, plus more for brushing

1 pound Swiss chard, rinsed

3 garlic cloves, minced

$1/4$ pound thinly sliced sopressata or Genoa salami

1 cup freshly grated Pecorino Romano cheese

1. Brush both sides of the bread with olive oil and set aside.

2. Trim the chard stems and cut crosswise into small pieces. Chop the leaves into $1/2$-inch strips. Heat the olive oil in a large sauté pan over medium heat. Sauté the stems until soft, about 10 minutes. Add the garlic and cook until fragrant but do not let it brown. Add the chopped leaves and toss to mix. Reduce the heat to low, cover, and cook for about 10 minutes. Toss occasionally until the leaves are wilted and turn dark green. Transfer the greens with a slotted spoon to a bowl.

3. Prepare a medium-hot gas or charcoal grill. Grill the bread until nicely browned on both sides and remove to a serving platter. (See Note for oven method.) Top each slice of bread with 1 or 2 pieces of sopressata, a generous amount of chard, and a sprinkle of cheese. Serve at once.

Note: Oven method for crostini: Preheat the oven to 350°F. Brush both sides of the bread with olive oil. Arrange the slices on 2 baking sheets. Bake until slightly dry on top, about 5 minutes. Turn and continue baking until crisp and golden brown, about 5 minutes.

Swiss chard leaves and roots contain phytonutrients, particularly anthocyans, which with fiber are especially helpful in preventing cancers of the digestive system. Eating Swiss chard reduces serum urea and creatinine levels, which may protect the kidneys of those with diabetes. Swiss chard helps maintain healthy bones by preventing osteoclast, which break bones down.

One cup of Swiss chard has approximately:

calories	35
carbohydrates	7.25g
fiber	3.68g
fat	.19g

Of the recommended daily value, this portion provides:

vitamin K	716%
vitamin A	110%
vitamin C	52%
vitamin E	16%
riboflavin	9%
vitamin B6	7%
thiamin	4%
magnesium	38%
manganese	29%
potassium	27%
copper	14%
sodium	13%
calcium	10%

Sautéed Swiss Chard and Chickpeas

Hearty greens and beans are a natural combination. Here we use chickpeas, but almost any type of bean will work well in this recipe. We also use canned chickpeas for convenience, but if you prefer cooked dried beans, by all means, use them.

makes 6 servings

2 tablespoons olive oil

1 medium red onion, thinly sliced

6 scallions (white and light green parts), trimmed and cut into 1-inch pieces

2 garlic cloves, thinly sliced

$^1/_2$ pound Swiss chard, rinsed, stemmed, and coarsely chopped

$^1/_2$ cup chicken broth, divided

Kosher salt and freshly ground black pepper

1 can (15 ounces) chickpeas, rinsed and drained

Pinch of red pepper flakes

2 tablespoons fresh lemon juice

$^1/_2$ cup chopped fresh flat-leaf parsley

1. In a large skillet, heat the oil over medium heat. Add the onion, scallions, and garlic and cook, stirring often, until softened, about 5 minutes.

2. Add the Swiss chard and toss well until coated. Add $^1/_4$ cup of the broth and salt and pepper to taste and cook, tossing well, until the chard is just wilted, about 5 minutes.

3. Add the chickpeas and the remaining $^1/_4$ cup broth and cook, stirring occasionally, for 2 minutes. Add the red pepper flakes, lemon juice, and parsley and cook, stirring often, for an additional 5 minutes. Serve at once.

Swiss Chard with Raisins and Pine Nuts

We like to use a mix of both red and white chard in this quick-cook dish.

makes 6 servings

2 tablespoons olive oil

1 cup finely chopped red onion

2 garlic cloves, thinly sliced

$\frac{1}{4}$ cup chicken or vegetable broth, or more to taste

$\frac{1}{3}$ cup golden raisins

2 bunches Swiss chard, preferably white and red,
  rinsed, stemmed, and coarsely chopped

Kosher salt and freshly ground black pepper

$\frac{1}{2}$ cup pine nuts, toasted

1. In a large skillet, heat the oil over medium heat. Add the onion and garlic and cook, stirring often, until softened, about 3 minutes. Add the broth and raisins, reduce the heat, and simmer for about 2 minutes. Add the chard and cook over high heat, tossing well, until the leaves are tender, 3 to 5 minutes. Add more broth if the mixture seems too dry. Season to taste with salt and pepper and toss again.

2. Transfer to a serving dish, sprinkle with the pine nuts, and serve at once.

Swiss Chard and Gruyère Gratin

This is an excellent side dish to serve with roasted or grilled meat. Be sure to include some of the chard stems in this dish—they add a nice crunch and flavor.

makes 4 to 6 servings

1 large bunch (about 1¹/₂ pounds) Swiss chard,
   rinsed and tough ends removed

3 teaspoons olive oil, divided

Kosher salt and freshly ground black pepper

1 cup freshly grated Gruyère cheese

2 tablespoons freshly grated Parmesan cheese

1. Preheat the oven to 350°F.

2. Cut the stems and leaves of the chard into 2-inch pieces. Put them in a large sauté pan and add 2 tablespoons of water. Cook over medium heat, tossing occasionally, until tender, about 5 minutes. Drain in a colander and let cool. Transfer the chard to a large bowl, add ¹/₂ tablespoon of the oil and salt and pepper to taste and toss.

3. Coat a gratin or baking dish with the remaining 1¹/₂ teaspoons oil. Arrange the chard in one layer and sprinkle the top with the cheeses. Add a bit of pepper, if desired. (The recipe can be prepared to this point a few hours ahead of time.)

4. Bake for 15 minutes and serve at once.

Swiss Chard and Cheese Frittata

Frittatas are so easy to make, and they're good to serve for breakfast or brunch hot from the oven or cooled to room temperature. This version, made with Swiss chard and cheese, is one of our favorites.

makes 6 servings

Cooking spray

1 pound Swiss chard, rinsed

2 tablespoons butter

1 small onion, finely chopped

7 eggs

1 cup shredded cheddar, Monterey Jack, or provolone cheese,
    or a mixture of any two

Kosher salt and freshly ground black pepper

1. Preheat the oven to 350°F. Coat a 2-quart baking dish with cooking spray and set aside.

2. Remove the stems from the Swiss chard and cut crosswise into thin slices. Stack the leaves, roll them up lengthwise, and slice crosswise into strips. Set aside.

3. Melt the butter over medium heat in a skillet or sauté pan with a lid. Add the onion and the chard stems and cook about 10 minutes until the onion is soft but not brown. Add the chard leaves to the pan; stir well and cover. The pan will look overstuffed, but the chard will wilt down rather quickly. Cook over low heat for about 8 minutes, tossing occasionally.

4. In a large bowl, beat the eggs until frothy. Add the cheese, cooked greens, and salt and pepper to taste, and mix well. Pour the mixture into the prepared pan and bake for 20 minutes.

5. Preheat the broiler. Broil the frittata until the top is lightly browned, 3 to 5 minutes. Let the frittata sit for about 10 minutes before serving. Slice into squares and serve directly from the baking dish or let cool to room temperature and serve.

Macaroni and Cheese with Swiss Chard

Mac 'n cheese is a favorite dish for adults and kids alike. In this recipe we add a layer of chopped Swiss chard to the delicious mix.

makes 6 servings

1¹/₂ pounds fresh Swiss chard, rinsed and stemmed

4 tablespoons (¹/₂ stick) unsalted butter

2 cups diced onions

¹/₄ cup unbleached all-purpose flour

3 cups warm whole milk

2 cups (about 8 ounces) grated sharp cheddar cheese

2 cups (about 8 ounces) grated Monterey Jack cheese

2 tablespoons Dijon mustard

¹/₂ teaspoon hot sauce

¹/₂ teaspoon ground nutmeg

Kosher salt and freshly ground black pepper

1 pound elbow macaroni, penne, or fusilli

4 tablespoons freshly grated Parmesan cheese

1. Preheat the oven to 350°F. Generously butter a 2-quart baking dish.

2. Bring a large pot of salted water to a boil. Cook the Swiss chard for 1 minute and drain. When cool enough to handle, squeeze out as much moisture as possible. Chop finely and set aside.

3. Melt the butter in a large saucepan over medium heat. Cook the onions until soft but not browned. Add the flour and cook for 2 minutes, stirring constantly. Whisk in the milk until thoroughly blended. Cook, whisking constantly, until the mixture begins to thicken. Remove from the heat, stir in the cheeses, mustard, hot sauce, nutmeg, and salt and pepper to taste.

4. Meanwhile, bring a large pot of salted water to a boil and cook the pasta until al dente. Drain and return to the pot. Add the cheese sauce and stir to blend well. Spoon half of the mixture into the prepared dish. Sprinkle with half of the Parmesan cheese. Top with the Swiss chard and smooth out. Top with the remaining macaroni mixture and Parmesan cheese. (The dish can be prepared up to this point and refrigerated, covered, up to 8 hours ahead of time. Bring to room temperature before baking.)

5. Bake until the mixture is hot and bubbling, about 30 minutes. Remove and turn on the broiler. Brown the macaroni and cheese under the broiler until the top is nicely browned, about 3 minutes. Serve at once.

Swiss Chard, Spinach, and Mushroom Torte

This torte is filled with greens, mushrooms, and cheese and has a nice buttery, free-form crust. Serve it with a salad and some crusty bread for a nice, homey supper.

makes 4 to 6 servings

crust:

2 cups unbleached all-purpose flour

Pinch of kosher salt

6 tablespoons cold unsalted butter, cut into pieces

2 eggs, separated

1 tablespoon olive oil

3 to 6 tablespoons cold water

filling:

2 tablespoons olive oil

1 cup chopped onion

1/2 pound mushrooms (such as button, cremini, or shiitake), stemmed and coarsely chopped

1 pound Swiss chard, rinsed, stemmed, and chopped

1 pound fresh spinach, rinsed, stemmed, and chopped

Kosher salt and freshly ground black pepper

2 eggs

1/2 cup freshly grated Asiago or Parmesan cheese, or a combination

1/4 cup pine nuts

1. To make the crust, combine the flour and salt in a food processor and pulse to mix. Add the butter and pulse until the mixture resembles coarse meal. Whisk together the egg yolks, olive oil, and 3 tablespoons of cold water and pour over the flour. Process briefly and add more water, 1 tablespoon at a time, until the dough holds together. Form the dough into a disk, wrap in plastic, and refrigerate for 30 minutes.

2. To make the filling, heat the olive oil in a large skillet over medium heat. Add the onion and cook until softened, 5 minutes. Add the mushrooms and cook until softened, 5 to 7 minutes. Add the Swiss chard and cook until wilted, 5 minutes. Add the spinach and cook until wilted, 3 minutes. Add salt and pepper to taste. Transfer to a large bowl and let cool.

3. Remove the dough from the refrigerator and roll out with a floured rolling pin on a lightly floured surface into a 16-inch circle. Fit the dough into a 9 x 3-inch springform pan, allowing the edge to drape over the side.

4. Whisk the eggs together and add to the greens mixture. Add the cheese and pine nuts and mix thoroughly. Spoon the filling into the dough-lined pan. Fold the dough toward the center of the torte; the filling in the center will be exposed. Brush the dough with the reserved egg whites and bake until nicely browned, about 45 minutes.

5. Remove from the oven and let rest for 10 minutes. Remove the side of the springform pan and slide onto a serving plate. Serve at once.

Mini Penne and Swiss Chard Stems with Cream Sauce

This is a very pretty dish that uses Swiss chard stems instead of the leaves. The little bit of crunch of the stems adds a surprising and tasty texture. We like to use mini penne pasta in this dish so the stems and the pasta are approximately the same size, but you can use any other type of small pasta. Save the chard leaves for adding to soups or egg dishes.

makes 6 servings

4 tablespoons (½ stick) butter

2 shallots, thinly sliced

3 cups Swiss chard stems (about 10 ounces),
   rinsed, cut lengthwise, and sliced on the diagonal into 1-inch pieces

¾ cup vegetable broth or water

1 pound mini penne or other small pasta

1 cup heavy cream

6 ounces fontina cheese, grated

Kosher salt and freshly ground black pepper

1. Melt the butter in a large sauté pan with a lid. Add the shallots and cook over medium heat until soft, about 3 minutes. Add the stems and sauté for 5 minutes. Add the broth, cover, and cook over low heat for another 10 minutes.

2. Meanwhile, cook the pasta according to package directions. Drain, reserving 1 cup of the cooking liquid.

3. Add the cream and cheese to the chard stems and stir until the cheese is melted. Do not let it boil. Add the pasta to the pan and stir until blended. If the mixture seems too thick, add a bit of the reserved cooking liquid to it. Season with salt and pepper to taste and serve at once.

watercress

Watercress is said to be one of the most ancient greens known to man. In antiquity the Persians, Greeks, and Romans widely used it for medicinal purposes. Its botanical name is *nasturtium officianale* and it is a member of the cruciferous family.

Watercress is widely available year-round. Look for bunches with fresh, dark green leaves and pass on any with wilted, yellowish leaves. It can be stored, unwashed, in a plastic bag in the refrigerator, but because of its high water content, watercress should be used within a few days after purchasing or picking.

Peppery watercress adds lovely flavor, color, and texture to all types of soups, salads, and sandwiches. It also makes a tasty fried appetizer, and it is excellent to sauté with a bit of oil, garlic, and lemon for a delicious, tangy side dish.

Fried Watercress
with Miso-Orange Dipping Sauce

Here's a great outdoor cocktail snack. Look for watercress leaves that have sturdy stems that can be used as a handle to pick up the fried watercress and dip it in the miso sauce.

makes 6 to 8 servings
miso-orange dipping sauce:
$1/4$ cup miso paste
2 tablespoons freshly squeezed orange juice
1 tablespoon soy sauce
2 tablespoons sweet mirin
1 teaspoon grated orange rind

Enough bunches of watercress to have at least 2 dozen sturdy stems
$1/2$ cup prepared tempura batter mix
$2/3$ cup water
Kosher salt
Canola oil, for frying

1. To make the dipping sauce, in a small bowl combine the miso paste, orange juice, soy sauce, mirin, and orange rind. Mix together until smooth. Add a bit more orange juice, if needed, to make a light sauce.

2. Choose the best pieces of watercress, ones that have a good amount of leaves and a sturdy long stem. Wash them and lay them out to dry between two clean dish towels.

3. Combine the tempura batter mix and water in a bowl. The batter should be thin but not watery so that the watercress leaves can be well coated.

4. Heat 2 to 3 inches of the oil in a heavy-bottomed pan until hot but not smoking, about 370°F on a candy thermometer. Using tongs, grab a stem and swish the leafy end around in the batter to coat. Let some of the batter drip off a bit and then lower it into the pot. Fry for about 15 seconds, until the batter is lightly browned. Transfer to a rack to drain for a few minutes, then arrange in a pile on a plate. Serve at once with the dipping sauce.

Creamy Watercress Soup

Served hot or cold, this creamy leek and potato-based soup tastes wonderful when fresh, peppery watercress is added to it. This versatile soup can also be made with other vegetables, such as asparagus, broccoli, or cauliflower.

makes 6 servings

2 tablespoons olive oil

1 tablespoon unsalted butter

1 leek (white and green part), rinsed and diced

2 cups thinly sliced onions (about 4 onions)

4 cups chicken broth, preferably homemade

4 cups water

6 russet potatoes, peeled and diced

1 cup milk

2 cups rinsed, stemmed, and finely chopped fresh watercress (about 2 bunches)

$1/_2$ teaspoon ground nutmeg

Kosher salt and freshly ground black pepper

3 tablespoons chopped flat-leaf parsley

1. In a large stockpot, heat the oil and butter over medium heat until the butter melts. Add the leek and onions and sauté for about 10 minutes, stirring occasionally, until tender. Add the broth, water, and potatoes and bring to a boil over high heat. Reduce the heat to medium low and simmer, covered, for 15 to 20 minutes, or until the potatoes are fork-tender. Cool for about 20 minutes.

2. Transfer the soup base to a food processor or blender and process until smooth. (This may have to be done in batches.)

3. Return the soup base to the pot, add the milk, and heat over medium heat, stirring, until hot. Add the watercress and nutmeg and season to taste with salt and pepper. Add the parsley and serve immediately.

Note: To serve cold, let the soup cool for about 30 minutes. Cover and refrigerate until cold. The base alone will keep in the refrigerator for up to 3 days and in the freezer for up to 1 month.

Sautéed Watercress and Garlic

Although watercress is a more delicate green than most others, it has a strong and assertive flavor when it is sautéed. This simple side dish is superb with salmon, or roast chicken or pork.

makes 6 servings

3 bunches fresh watercress

2 tablespoons olive oil

2 garlic cloves, thinly sliced

Kosher salt and freshly ground black pepper

1 teaspoon fresh lemon juice

1. Remove the large stems from the watercress and rinse well in several changes of cold water. Spin dry in a salad spinner or on a clean towel.

2. Heat the oil in a large skillet over medium heat. Add the garlic and cook until just softened, 2 to 3 minutes. Add the watercress, one bunch at a time, to the pan. Toss well with tongs until the watercress is completely wilted. Add salt and pepper to taste, sprinkle with lemon juice, and serve at once.

Watercress has more calcium than milk and more vitamin C than oranges. Eating watercress daily can significantly reduce DNA damage to blood cells, which is considered to be an important trigger in the development of cancer.

One cup of fresh watercress has approximately:

calories	3.7
carbohydrates	.4g
protein	0.8g
fat	0

Of the recommended daily value, this portion provides:

vitamin A	22%
vitamin C	24%
vitamin E	2%
vitamin K	106%
vitamin B6	2%
folate	1%
pantothenic acid	1%
calcium	4%
magnesium	2%
manganese	4%
potassium	3%
phosphorous	2%
copper	1%

Egg and Watercress Salad Toasts

Fresh watercress transforms ordinary egg salad into something very special and tasty. For a wonderful outdoor lunch, serve a platter of these open-faced sandwiches with vegetable crudités, pickles, and iced tea.

makes 6 servings

1/2 pound watercress

6 eggs

2 scallions (white and green parts), minced

2 tablespoons mayonnaise

1 teaspoon fresh lemon juice

Kosher salt

Buttered toast, for serving

1. Remove the large stems from the watercress and rinse well in several changes of cold water. Spin dry in a salad spinner or on a clean towel. Chop the watercress and transfer to a large bowl.

2. Put the eggs in a large pot and cover with cold water to about an inch above the eggs. Cook over high heat until it comes to a boil. Remove from the burner, cover, and let stand for 15 minutes. Place the eggs in a bowl filled with ice water and let stand until completely cool.

3. Peel and chop the eggs and add to the bowl of watercress. Add the scallions, mayonnaise, lemon juice, and salt to taste and mix well. Taste and adjust the seasonings, adding a bit more mayonnaise if necessary. Serve on buttered toast.

zucchini

Zucchini is a summer squash that is, botanically speaking, an immature fruit and not a vegetable. It was developed in Northern Italy in the late nineteenth century and was introduced to this country by Italian immigrants in the 1920s.

Because zucchini is a fast and easy grower, it has a reputation among home gardeners for its overwhelming production. It is available all year and at its best in late spring through early fall. Look for zucchini that is fairly small, no more than eight inches, and that is firm and heavy. The skin should be tender and thin. Pass on any zucchini that have soft spots or bruises. It will keep in a plastic bag in the refrigerator for about three days and should be free of moisture before storing.

Zucchini is an important vegetable to many cuisines, including Italian, French, and Greek, to name just a few. We love its versatility and use it to make great appetizers like caponata and pancakes. And for an amazing springtime treat, we stuff and fry its delicate flowers. We also make it into soup, sauté it, grill it, and add it to pasta dishes. These are all good reasons to celebrate the abundance of zucchini!

Chilled Zucchini and Herb Soup

Cold and creamy zucchini soup, flavored with lemon zest, garden-fresh parsley, basil, and paprika has a fresh, smooth taste. This is a wonderful way to begin a summer meal.

makes 6 servings

2 tablespoons olive oil

$1/2$ cup shallots, thinly sliced

4 medium zucchini, peeled, halved lengthwise,
   and cut into $1/4$-inch slices

1 tablespoon lemon zest

Kosher salt and freshly ground black pepper

$2^1/_2$ cups chicken or vegetable broth

$1^1/_2$ cups water

1 cup chopped fresh flat-leaf parsley, plus more for garnish

2 tablespoons chopped fresh basil, plus more for garnish

1 teaspoon paprika

Dash of hot sauce

$1/2$ cup plain yogurt

Lemon slices, for garnish

1. In a large soup pot, heat the oil over medium heat. Cook the shallots, stirring occasionally, until softened, about 5 minutes.

2. Add the zucchini, lemon zest, and salt and pepper to taste and cook, stirring occasionally, until the zucchini is softened, about 7 minutes. Add the broth and water and bring to a boil. Reduce the heat and simmer until the zucchini is very tender, about 10 minutes. Set aside to cool.

3. Transfer the mixture to a blender. Add the parsley, basil, paprika, and hot sauce and blend until very smooth. This may have to be done in batches. Pour the mixture into a bowl, add the yogurt, and mix well. Chill, covered in the refrigerator, for up to 4 hours or overnight.

4. Before serving, stir well. Taste and adjust the seasonings, if necessary. Serve the soup garnished with additional parsley and basil and lemon slices.

Zucchini Caponata

Caponata is usually made with eggplant, but our zucchini version is quite excellent too. The zucchini is sautéed until golden and then onions, celery, tomatoes, capers, and olives are slowly cooked with it. It makes a wonderful hors d'oeuvre served with crispy pita bread, and it's also very good with grilled lamb or steak.

makes 6 servings

3 medium zucchini

3 tablespoons olive oil, divided

1 red onion, chopped

1 cup chopped celery
(about 4 stalks)

1 cup canned plum tomatoes,
coarsely chopped,
with their juices

1 tablespoon balsamic vinegar

1 tablespoon capers

$1/2$ cup kalamata olives,
pitted and chopped

1 teaspoon sugar

Freshly ground black pepper

1. Trim and quarter the zucchini lengthwise and cut into $1/2$-inch pieces.

2. Heat 2 tablespoons of the oil over medium heat. In a large skillet, sauté the zucchini, stirring occasionally, until golden, about 10 minutes. Remove with a slotted spoon and set aside.

3. Add the remaining 1 tablespoon oil to the pan and reduce the heat. Add the onion and cook until softened, about 3 minutes. Add the celery and cook until tender, about 10 minutes. Add the tomatoes and their juices and cook, stirring occasionally, for 10 minutes. Add the zucchini, vinegar, capers, olives, sugar, and pepper to taste and simmer over low heat, stirring occasionally, for 10 minutes. Taste and adjust the seasonings, if necessary. Serve at once or chill for a few hours or overnight and serve cold or at room temperature. The caponata will keep, in the refrigerator, covered, for five days.

Fried Stuffed Zucchini Flowers

Zucchini flowers are the golden blossoms that grow on the ends of baby zucchini plants. When they are stuffed with cheese, dipped in batter, and lightly fried, they are deliciously addictive. We like to serve these springtime treats hot with cold beer.

makes 4 to 6 servings
12 large zucchini blossoms
3 ounces fontina, mozzarella, or Havarti cheese
1½ cups prepared tempura batter mix
Corn or canola oil, for frying
Kosher salt

1. Open the top of each blossom and carefully remove the stamen inside the flower. Rinse under cold water and lay out on a clean towel to dry for at least 1 hour.

2. Cut the cheese into 1-inch long pieces. Open the end of the flower again and place a piece of cheese inside each flower. Twist the end of each flower to keep the cheese enclosed. Mix the tempura batter mix according to package directions and set aside.

3. Heat 1-inch of oil in a deep sauté pan until hot but not smoking. Dip each blossom into the batter holding onto the twisted end. Carefully lay the blossoms on their sides in the hot oil. Fry for 30 seconds. Turn and fry for 30 more seconds, or until golden brown and the cheese is melted. Drain on a wire rack. Sprinkle with salt to taste and serve.

Zucchini is an excellent source of manganese and vitamins A and C, and it is very low in calories. Zucchini skin contains most of its nutrients and the darker the skin, the greater the amount of the nutrients.

One cup of boiled zucchini has approximately:

calories	29
carbohydrates	7.1g
protein	1.2g
fat	0.1g

Of the recommended daily value, this portion provides:

vitamin A	40%
vitamin C	14%
vitamin E	1%
vitamin K	9%
vitamin B6	7%
folate	8%
niacin	4%
pantothenic acid	2%
calcium	4%
iron	4%
magnesium	10%
manganese	16%
potassium	13%
phosphorous	7%
copper	8%
selenium	1%

Zucchini Pancakes

Zucchini pancakes offer another solution to what to do with those huge zucchini plants in your vegetable garden. Like cooking potato pancakes, there is a trick to making them crisp and not soggy. All of the moisture must be squeezed out of the zucchini before mixing it with the other ingredients. This requires the use of a thirsty kitchen towel or two and some elbow grease—but the results are well worth it. These light and crispy pancakes make a delicious side dish or a light vegetarian supper.

makes about 12 pancakes

3 medium zucchini, peeled and shredded

Kosher salt

3 eggs, lightly beaten

1 tablespoon olive oil

$1/2$ cup crumbled feta cheese

$1/4$ cup freshly grated Parmesan cheese

2 scallions, trimmed and minced

Dash of hot sauce

Kosher salt and freshly ground black pepper

$1/2$ cup all-purpose unbleached flour

1 teaspoon baking powder

$1/2$ cup canola or safflower oil, for frying

1. Put the zucchini in a colander, sprinkle with salt, and let drain for 30 minutes. Transfer to a kitchen towel. Squeeze out as much moisture as possible.

2. In a large mixing bowl, combine the zucchini and eggs. Add the oil, feta cheese, Parmesan cheese, scallions, hot sauce, and salt and pepper to taste and mix well with a fork.

3. Sift the flour and baking powder together and stir into the zucchini mixture and mix well.

4. Heat about $1/4$ cup of the oil in a large cast-iron skillet or other heavy skillet over medium heat until hot but not smoking. Drop a few heaping tablespoons of the zucchini batter into the pan, allowing room for them to spread. Flatten with a spatula if necessary. They should be $2^{1}/2$ to 3 inches in diameter. Fry until lightly browned on one side. Turn over and fry until lightly browned on other side. Repeat once or twice until the pancakes are crisp, frying about 8 minutes total.

5. Transfer to a plate lined with paper towels and keep warm in a low oven while cooking the remaining pancakes. Continue frying with the remaining batter, adding more oil as needed. Serve at once.

Linguini with Zucchini and Onions

In this fantastic dish, slow-cooked zucchini and onions become a sweet and creamy sauce to mix with pasta, cheese, and freshly toasted breadcrumbs. If you prefer a chunkier style of sauce, slice the zucchini into half-rounds instead of grating them. This is Liz's son Eddie's favorite dish.

makes 6 servings

4 medium zucchini (about 1½ pounds), coarsely grated

¼ cup olive oil

1 large or 2 medium yellow onions, thinly sliced into ½-inch rounds

¼ cup kosher salt

1 pound linguini

½ cup freshly grated Parmesan cheese

½ cup fresh breadcrumbs

1. Put the zucchini in a colander over a bowl and drain for about 30 minutes.

2. Heat the oil in a sauté pan large enough to hold the vegetables and cooked pasta. Add the onions and cook over very low heat, stirring occasionally, until they begin to caramelize, about 30 minutes. Add the zucchini and mix well. Cover and cook for 20 minutes, stirring occasionally. The vegetable mixture will become very soft and sauce-like.

3. Bring a large pot of water to boil. Add the salt and linguini and cook until al dente. Drain the pasta, reserving 2 cups of the pasta water. Add the pasta to the sauce and toss well to coat. Add the reserved pasta water and let simmer until the water is absorbed and the pasta is cooked but not mushy, about 2 minutes. Add the cheese and toss well to coat.

4. Meanwhile, heat the broiler. Spread the breadcrumbs on a baking sheet and toast under the broiler until just browned. Be careful not to burn them.

5. Transfer the pasta mixture to a large platter, sprinkle with the toasted breadcrumbs, and serve at once.

Zucchini Parmesan

When we think of a Parmesan we usually think of the classic dish of layered eggplant, cheese, and tomato sauce. Here's a great variation that uses zucchini. We think it's a perfect recipe for the zucchini that was somehow overlooked in the garden and is now as big as your leg. The zucchini slices have to dry overnight, so plan accordingly.

makes 6 to 8 servings
1 large zucchini
Olive oil, for brushing
Kosher salt and freshly ground black pepper
2 to 3 cups tomato sauce
8 ounces provolone cheese, thinly sliced
¼ cup dry breadcrumbs
¼ cup freshly grated Parmesan cheese

1. Slice the zucchini lengthwise into ¼-inch-thick slices. Lay them out in a single layer on a rack and let dry overnight.

2. Preheat the broiler. Brush the zucchini slices with olive oil, add salt and pepper to taste, and put them on a baking sheet. Broil until lightly browned and then turn to brown the other side, about 3 minutes per side.

3. Reduce the oven temperature to 350°F.

4. Spoon a bit of the tomato sauce over the bottom of a 9 x 12-inch baking dish or casserole. Arrange the zucchini slices in a single layer. You may need to cut them to fit the dish. Top with a slightly overlapping layer of provolone cheese and spread a few tablespoons of tomato sauce over the cheese. Repeat the layering of zucchini, provolone cheese, and tomato sauce twice, ending with the tomato sauce. Mix the breadcrumbs and Parmesan cheese together in a small bowl and sprinkle over the top.

5. Bake for 30 minutes, until it is bubbling and the top is browned. Let stand at room temperature for 15 minutes before serving.

acknowledgments

To Angela Miller, who did what she does best—she made this book happen.

To Geoffrey Stone at Running Press, for his good suggestions, his editing skills, and for keeping the book on track.

To Colin Cooke, for his beautiful food and market photography and for being so much fun to work with. To Ulf Agger, for his wonderful food styling, and for letting us shoot in his great home and backyard.

To Charles Clough for his inspiring vegetable and garden photography and to Mark Ruisi—muse and magical garden designer.

To Barbara's family, Lester, Zan, and Isabelle, and friends for their support and enthusiasm and who ate more greens than they ever thought they could.

And to Liz's man, Charlie, the best sous chef. Thanks for keeping the knives sharp!

Photography Credits
Photographs by Colin Cooke: *Pages 9, 21, 24, 30, 34, 37, 48, 55, 57, 59, 66, 73, 81, 83, 84, 85, 96, 102–103, 118, 126-133, 139, 141, 143, 147, 154, 157, 165, 168, 172, 179 (right), 181, 186-187, 194, 195, 202, 213, 222, 224, 233.*

Photographs by Charles Clough: *Pages i, ii, 2-3, 6, 8, 10, 12, 15, 39, 41, 51, 52–53, 100, 111, 122, 123, 124, 134, 137, 148, 150, 179 (left), 184-185, 190, 191, 204, 207, 208, 216, 224, 228, 229.*

index